HOW TO BUILD
SHIP MODELS
A BEGINNER'S GUIDE

Written and Illustrated by A. Richard Mansir

FOREWORD

Herman Melville wrote in the opening chapter of Moby Dick,

"Posted like sentinels all around the town, stand thousands upon thousands of mortal men fixed in ocean reveries . . . Strange! Nothing will content them but the extremist limit of the land; . . . they must get just as nigh the water as they possibly can without falling in. And there they stand—miles of them—leagues . . . Tell me, does the magnetic virtue of the needles of the compasses of all those ships attract them thither?"

Perhaps this explains the unique fascination that goes along with the hobby of shipmodelling. Certainly no other craft has held the imagination of men in quite the same way since the first primitive canoe was launched thousands of years ago.

Tombs of the Egyptian pharoahs contained shipmodels and the islanders of the south seas built replicas of their catamarans. Europeans, from the days of ancient Greece, consistently recreated their ships in miniature.

Shipmodelling uniquely involves one in the entire history of man's adventure on earth, and in the evolution of one of his oldest and noblest engineering achievements. Railroads and airplanes are late comers, the product of but a single century, while ships were born long before the beginnings of recorded history.

The one who sets out on his first shipmodelling project has an endlessly intriguing experience ahead of him. The history and romance of the sea becomes real in his imagination, while a fine work of art comes to life under his hand.

This book has been written as an introduction to the art of shipmodelling. Writing it has been rather like a seagull trying to eat a whale. The feast is huge while the belly is small.

The morsels presented have been pecked out of the back of the beast here and there in the hope that they will make a tastyhors d'oeuvre. The reader, perhaps having tasted here, will want to stay for dinner.

The book deals largely with sailing ships of European or American vintage. These ships occupy a significant amount of our maritime heritage and continue to be the favorite subjects of model enthusiasts. The approach has been to present in a general way the major components of these ships with an emphasis on nomenclature and function. The objective has been to shed light on some aspects of ship construction and operation often left unclear or undefined in model plans.

Modelling techniques are suggested for certain parts throughout the book, more to spur the craftsman's imagination than to present definitive solutions. There are, after all, almost as many methods for building a ship model as there are shipmodellers. The examples given, however, may serve to convey the standard of craftsmanship common in fine ship models and hopefully lead the beginner to set a goal of excellence for himself.

This book is not a full meal off the whale's back. It is intended to supplement the plans and instructions that normally accompany a ship model kit, and otherwise point the way toward the ocean of historical and technical information that comprise the art of shipmodelling.

TABLE OF CONTENTS

Santa Maria

Sovereign of the Seas

Spanish Galleon

Whaler

Tug boat

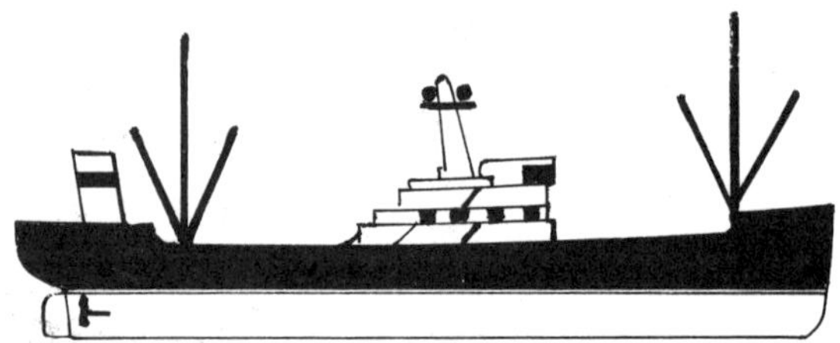

Freighter

Cutty Sark

Sloop

Yawl

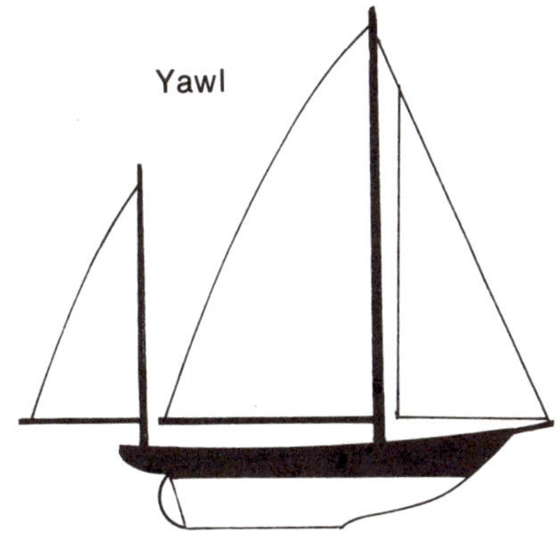

Ketch

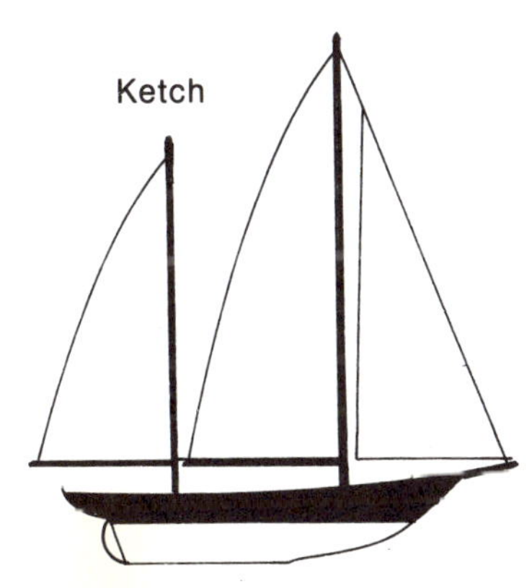

Schooner

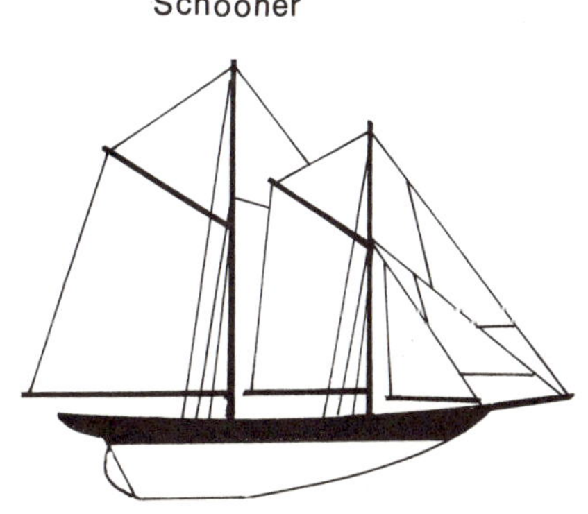

Brigantine

Brig

Bark

Full Rigged Ship

INTRODUCTION TO NAUTICAL TERMS

Nautical terminology is a technical vocabulary that has evolved through the centuries of man's seagoing history. English nautical terms, I suspect, had their origins in the early English, Norse, and Celtic languages as they were spoken in the years before Christ.

Each language of the world has a nautical vocabulary of similar antiquity.

Nautical terms are sometimes confusing to the initiate. Often the same word is used to denote several different things. The word "tack" is an example. Tack in one context means the side of the ship against which the wind is blowing; in another a maneuver in which the ship steers a zig-zag course into the wind; in a third, a rigging line; and finally the fore corner of a fore and aft sail. The key to meaning is context.

Spelling is sometimes confusing too. Through most of history the seaman's lingo was almost exclusively a spoken language. When literate men took on the task of writing out the vocabulary they were dependent on the sailors' pronunciations which could vary substantially depending on the inclination of the moment. For example the word "trennel" was also pronounced "trunnel." Literally a trennel was a "tree nail," a hard wood dowel used to pin a ship's planks to its frames. The phonetic spelling "trennel" reflects the casual, foreshortened pronunciation one might expect from an unlettered man of the sea. Fo'c'sle for forecastle is another example. There are many terms that reflect similar foundations.

None of this should dismay the beginning ship-modeller, however. By the time his first project is complete, the modeller can expect to have a vocabulary as salty as the saltiest of salts.

The basic terms on the next few pages plus the terms presented throughout this book will be enough to get one's sea legs going.

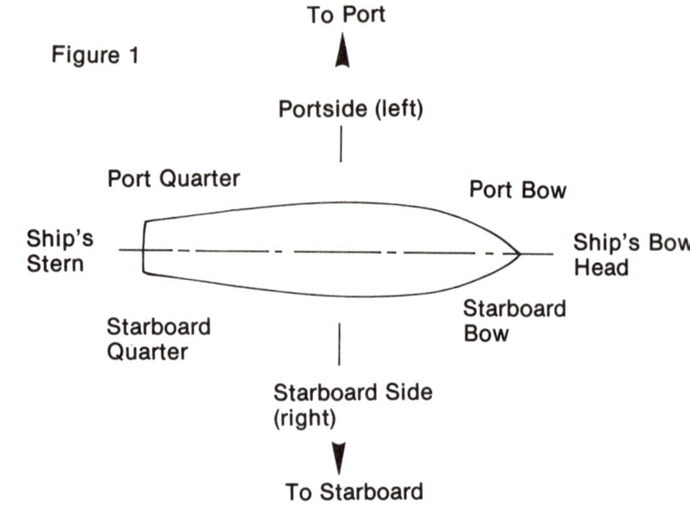

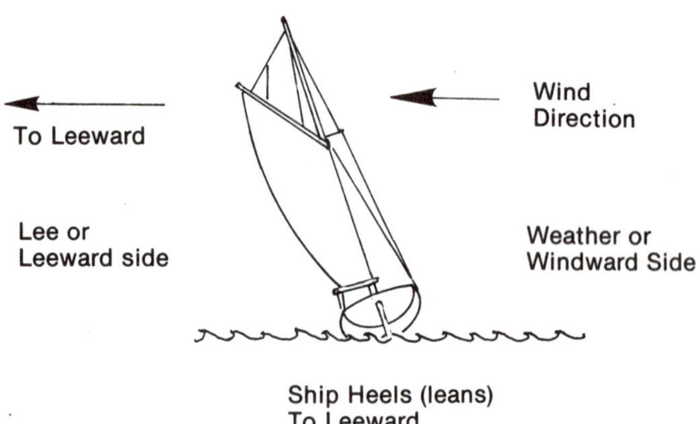

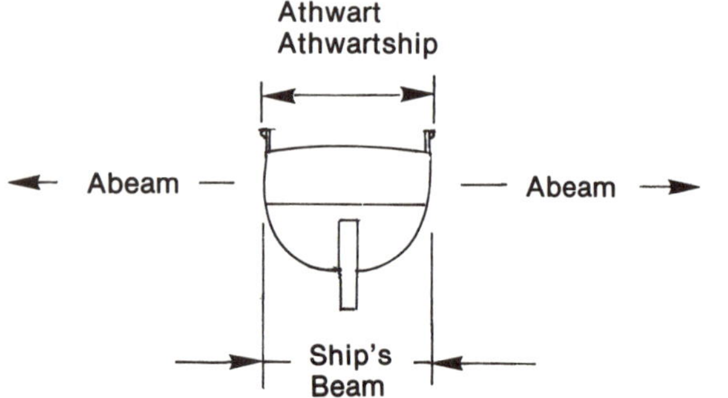

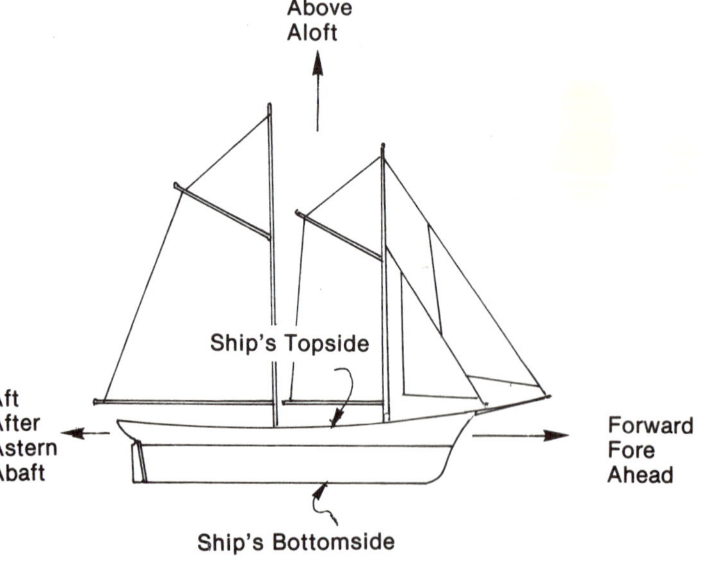

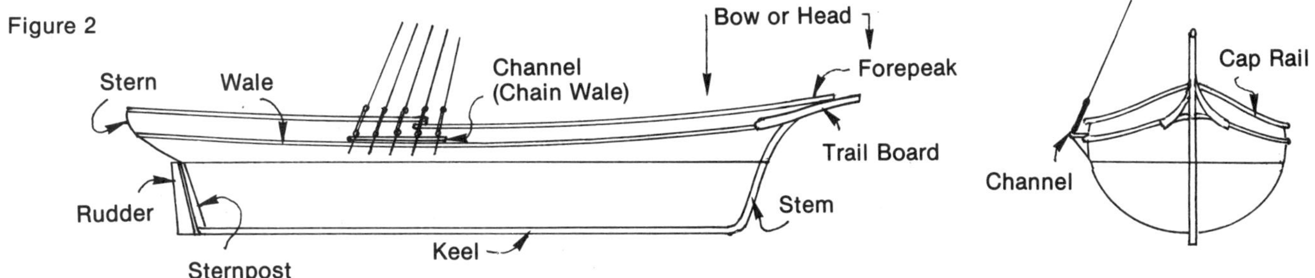
Figure 2
Bow or Head
Forepeak
Channel (Chain Wale)
Stern
Wale
Trail Board
Rudder
Stem
Sternpost
Keel
Cap Rail
Channel

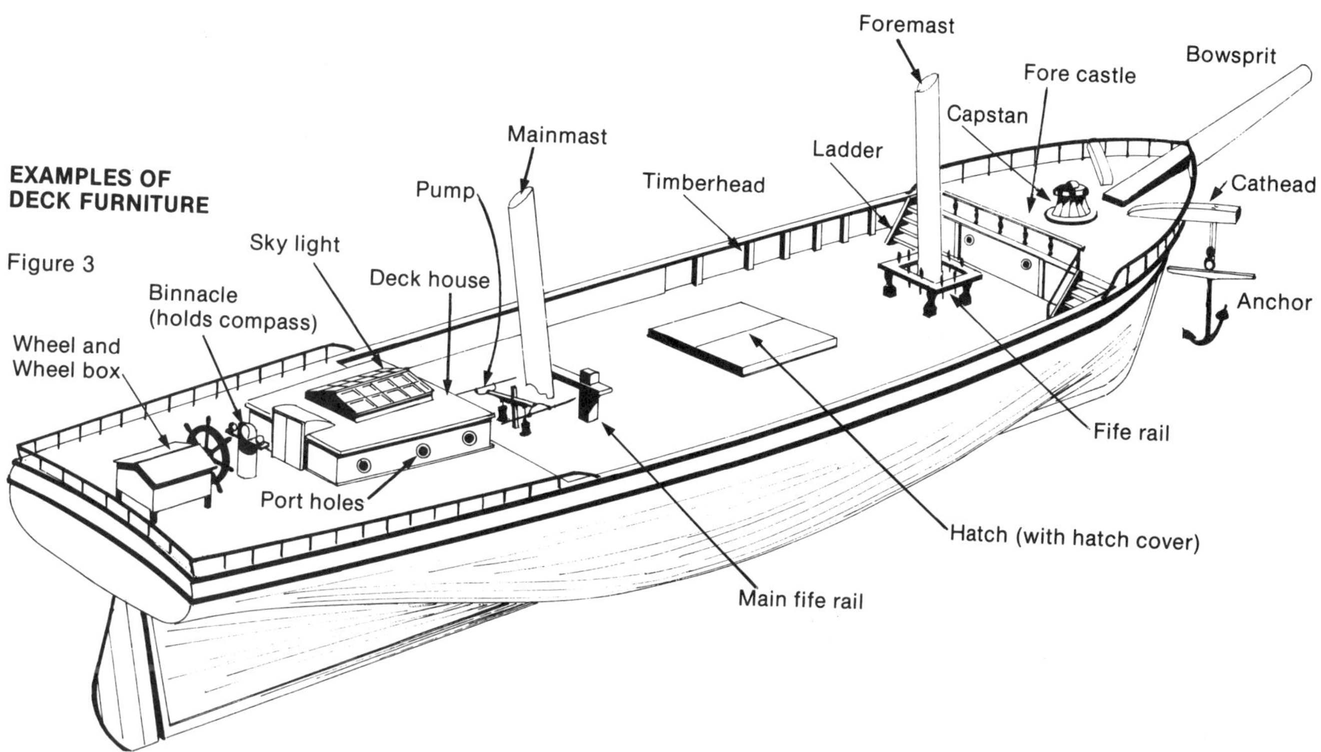
EXAMPLES OF DECK FURNITURE
Figure 3
Foremast
Fore castle
Bowsprit
Capstan
Mainmast
Ladder
Pump
Timberhead
Cathead
Sky light
Deck house
Binnacle (holds compass)
Anchor
Wheel and Wheel box
Fife rail
Port holes
Hatch (with hatch cover)
Main fife rail

Figure 4
Quarter Gallery
Head Rails
Poop Deck
Fore Deck
Quarter Deck
Main Deck
Taffrail
Orlop Deck (lowest deck)
Cheeks
Poop
Quarter
Main
Orlop

SAILING TERMS

Figure 5
A ship's compass rose

Figure 6
COURSE is the direction of
the ship

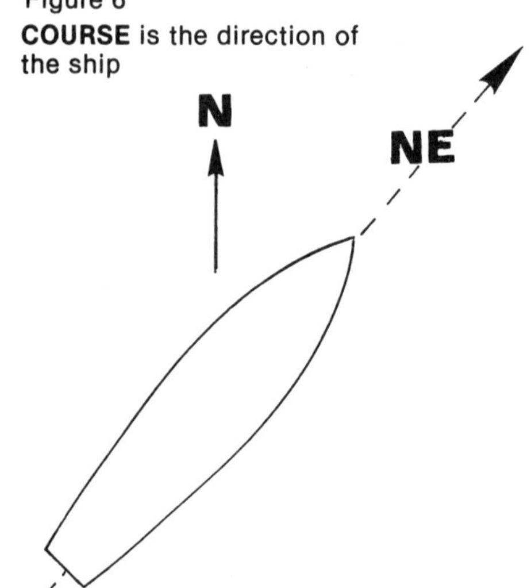

A compass heading is also
the ship's course
Ex. This ship is heading
northeast—her course
is northeast

Sailing ships are rigged so that sails can be trimmed to various wind conditions. Sailing "wind abeam" means that the ship is headed so that the wind is coming straight against her side. This is called a reach or reaching. When the wind blows from dead astern the ship is running or running before the wind. When a ship is sailing as straight into the wind as she can go and still make headway, she is said to be "beating up" or "beating to windward" while her sails in this situation will be "close hauled". If her head is pointing straight into the wind and she is going nowhere, she is "hove to" and her sails will be "aback" or "on the luff".

Changing a ship's course changes her relationship to the wind direction. If the ship steers so that the wind moves from one side of the ship to the other she is said to "change her tack". A ship on the starboard tack takes the wind over her starboard rail; on the port tack over the port rail.

To "come about" means to change the ship's tack by steering first into the wind and then "falling off" again on the new tack. To "jibe" the ship means to change the ship's tack by steering first downwind. Wearing a ship is the same maneuver as a jibe but applies to square riggers.

These and other sailing terms are useful to the modeller in helping him understand the "why" of the various gear he is modelling. For example, if you know that a ship's yardarms must be able to swing around to almost a full, fore and aft position, then you will not rig the model in such a way that this could never be done. Many beginners have made just this mistake.

Figure 7

Ship on **PORT TACK**—wind
blows over port rail

Ship on **STARBOARD TACK**—wind blows over
starboard rail

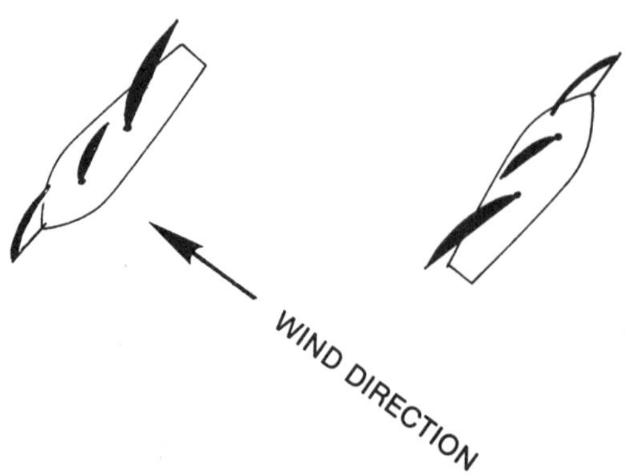

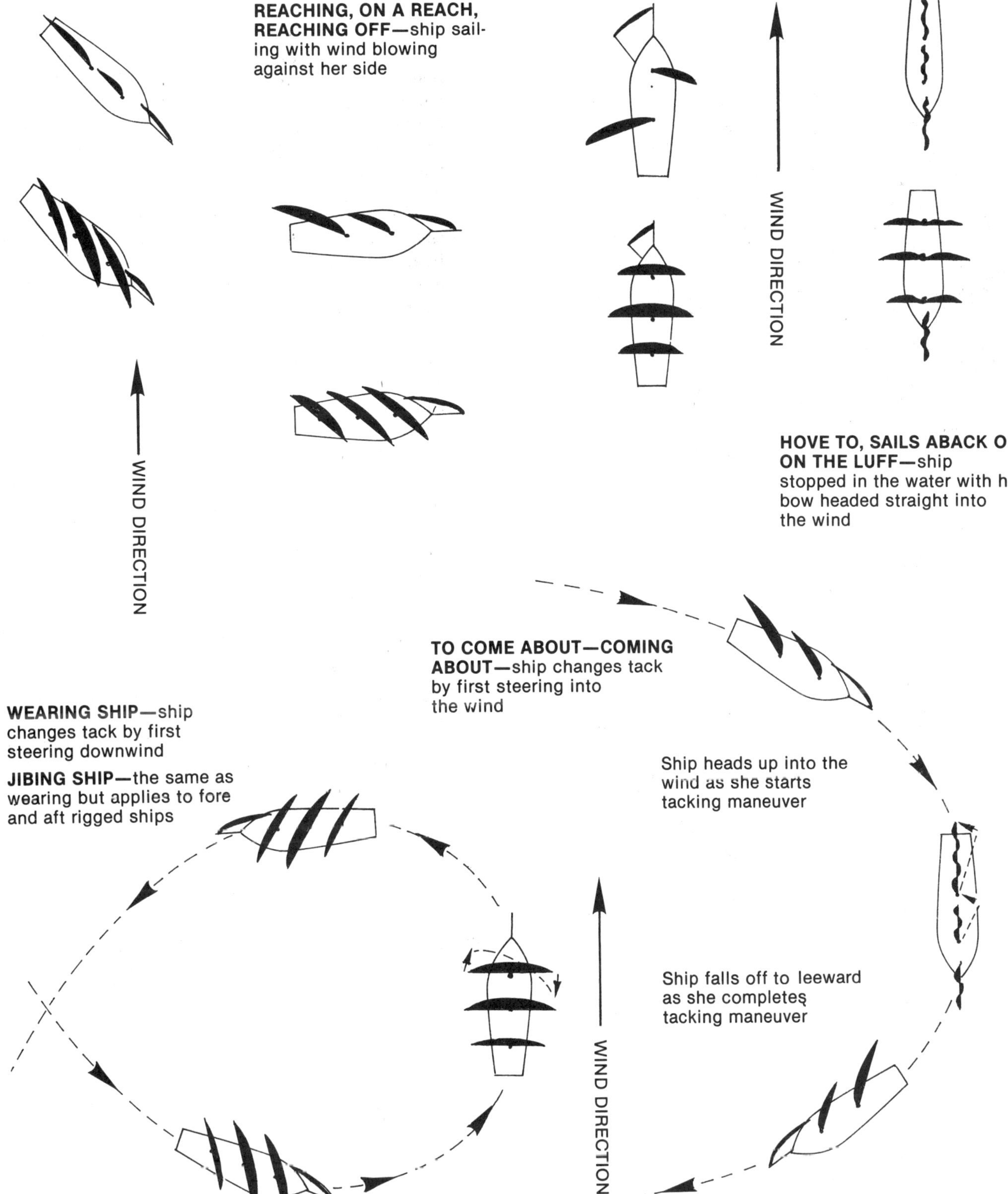

BEATING—ON A BEAT—
BEATING UP—ship sailing
into wind as much
as possible

REACHING, ON A REACH,
REACHING OFF—ship sail-
ing with wind blowing
against her side

RUNNING, RUNNING
BEFORE THE WIND, BROAD
OFF—ship sailing with the
wind dead behind her

WIND DIRECTION

WIND DIRECTION

HOVE TO, SAILS ABACK OR
ON THE LUFF—ship
stopped in the water with her
bow headed straight into
the wind

TO COME ABOUT—COMING
ABOUT—ship changes tack
by first steering into
the wind

Ship heads up into the
wind as she starts
tacking maneuver

WEARING SHIP—ship
changes tack by first
steering downwind

JIBING SHIP—the same as
wearing but applies to fore
and aft rigged ships

Ship falls off to leeward
as she completes
tacking maneuver

WIND DIRECTION

Figure 8

A SHIP'S LINES

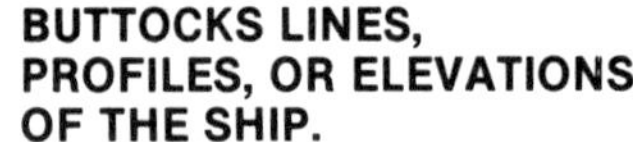

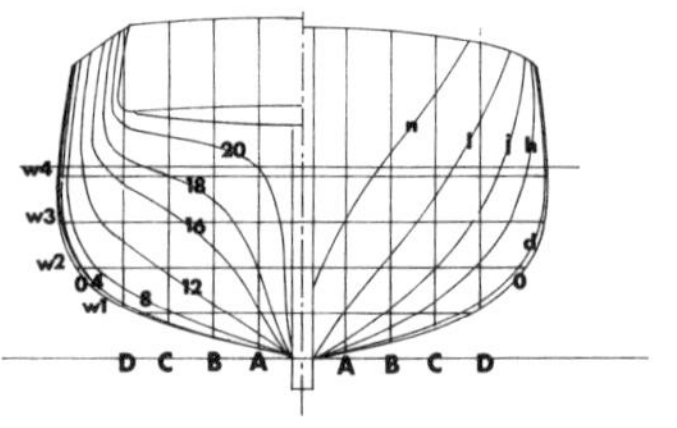

Numbered sections to the left show the after part of the ship; Lettered sections to the right show the fore part.

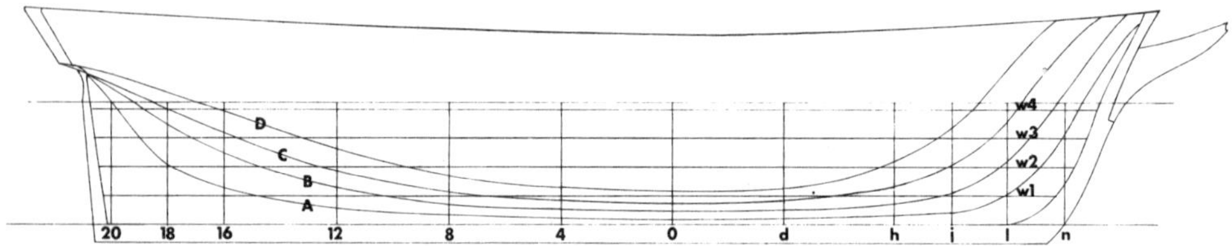

Figure 9

The hull of a ship is a subtle piece of sculpture. It is a three dimensional form with a surface of compound curves. The design of the hull shape is the challenge of marine architecture since it has everything to do with the ship's performance. Among other things, the hull shape determines the speed, manueverability, displacement, payload, stability, and rig, and influences the kind and amount of material to be used in its construction. A fine ship model is, a true and perfect rendering of this precisely engineered form. It is important, therefore, that you understand how to read and use the ship's "lines" that are included in your plans.

The lines are the marine architect's method of describing a three dimensional hull on a piece of two dimensional paper. The lines are really a "topographic map" of the ship's surface. (The word "topography" means the graphic description of a surface). The "map" may be understood by imagining that the three dimensional hull has been sliced up into a series of slabs, first one way, then another. The contours of these slabs, when traced off on paper are the lines you see in the drawings. The first series of slabs cut the hull from top to bottom across the width of the ship and yield the "body sections" or "sections" of the ship. The second set of slabs cut the ship up and down the long way parallel to its keel and yield the "buttocks", "sheer lines" or "profiles". A third set of lines is produced by slicing the ship the long way parallel to the plane of the water. These lines logically enough are called the "water lines". Finally, your plans may have one or two lines called "diagonals" which show the curve produced when the hull is cut stem to stern at an angle to the water lines. The latter are refinements that are used in full scale marine architecture but are not always included in model plans. In any event, they are not as vital to the modelling task as the sections, profiles and water lines and may be safely ignored.

Study the lines of your hull carefully. Now that you understand what the lines mean you should begin to see the dimensional form almost growing off the paper. The use of the hull lines in actual construction will be dealt with later.

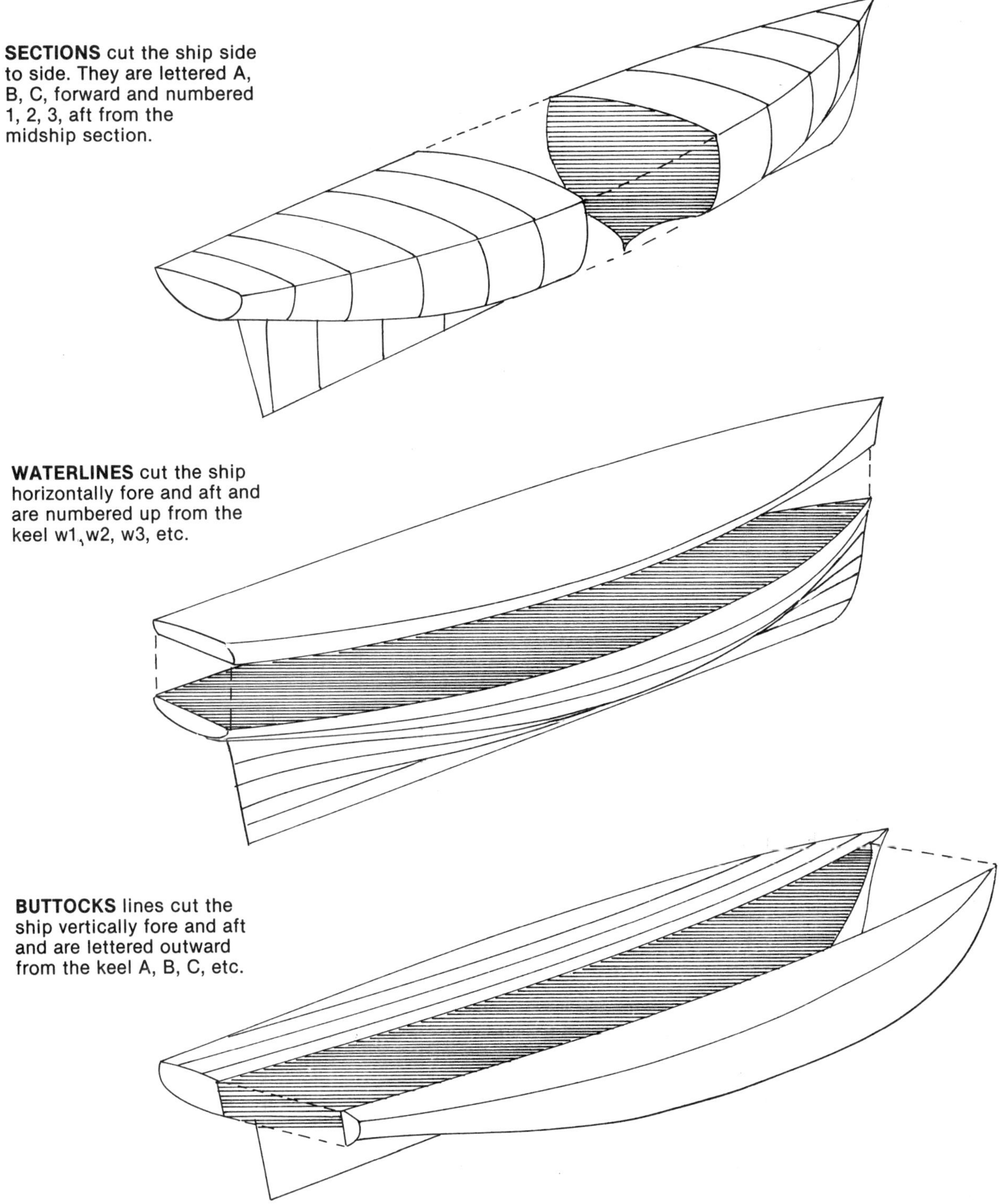

SECTIONS cut the ship side to side. They are lettered A, B, C, forward and numbered 1, 2, 3, aft from the midship section.
WATERLINES cut the ship horizontally fore and aft and are numbered up from the keel w1, w2, w3, etc.
BUTTOCKS lines cut the ship vertically fore and aft and are lettered outward from the keel A, B, C, etc.

Figure 10

THE HULL

There are several ways to model the hull of your ship. Which way you choose will depend on what your kit calls for, or how far you want to approximate the building methods of the full scale ship. Take your pick. The closer you get to the real ship's construction, the tougher the modelling job.

Many kits are furnished with a wooden block hull cut pretty close to the model's lines. These preformed blocks require only a minimum of carving to complete. (Figure 11)

CARVING A HULL

Trace off the profile of the ship on one side of the block. The profile may be cut either to the top of the bulwarks or to the top of the deck with allowance for the thickness of the cap rail or decking.

Cutting to the top of the bulwarks requires gouging out the block down to the deck level. (Figure 12.) Cutting to the deck level requires building up the bulwarks with sheet material. (Figure 23.) If you cut to the level of the deck remember that the deck has a camber, a side to side curve, (figure 26), and will be higher at the center line then along the sides.

Saw out the profile with a band or coping saw.

Trace off the widest waterlines on the bottom of the block with the keel in the center, and saw them out.

Carve down the stern sections after sketching in the shape of the transom with a pencil. As your carving gets close to looking right, cut section templates from some stiff material and use them as guides to your finished carving.

Carve the bow sections the same way and finally file and sand the hull clean and smooth. (Figure 13).

Cut the keel, stem and stern posts from sheet material. Glue and pin them to the hull. Figure 14.

Screw a working base to the bottom of the hull so that you can hold the model in a vise. Figure 15.

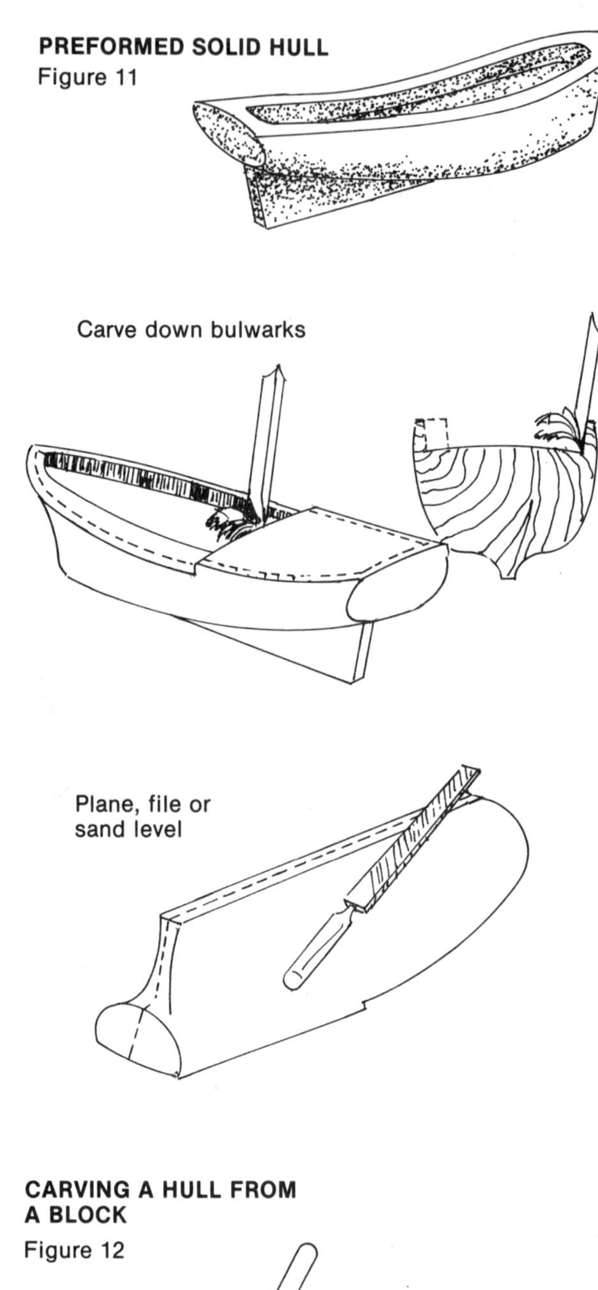

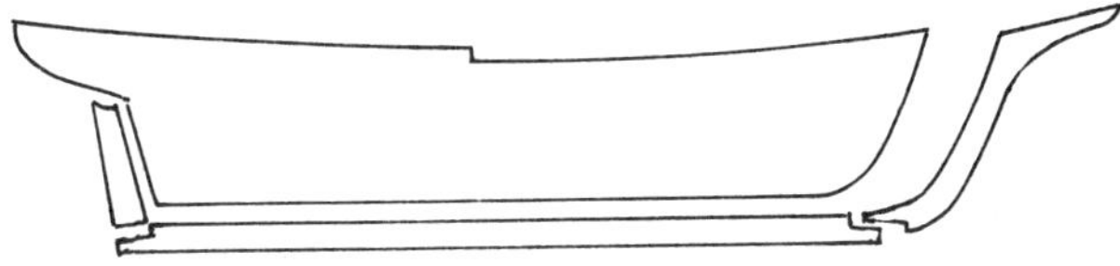

Add keel, stem, and rudder post

Figure 14

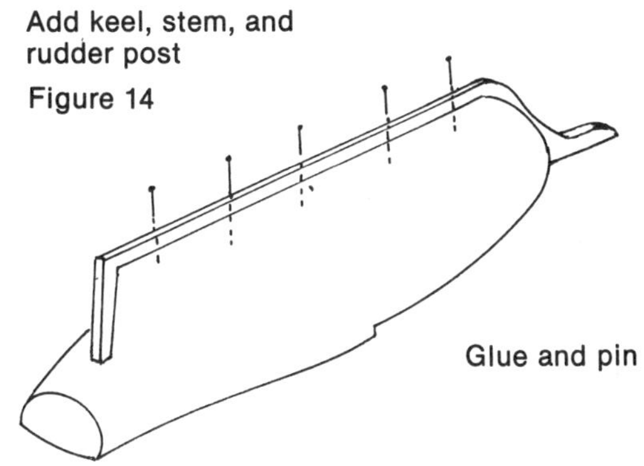

Glue and pin

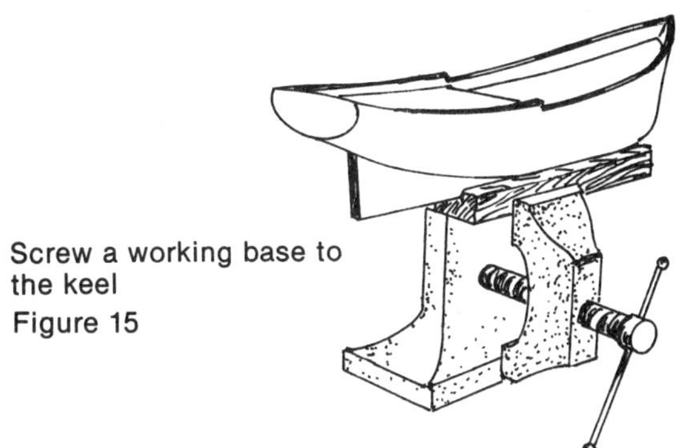

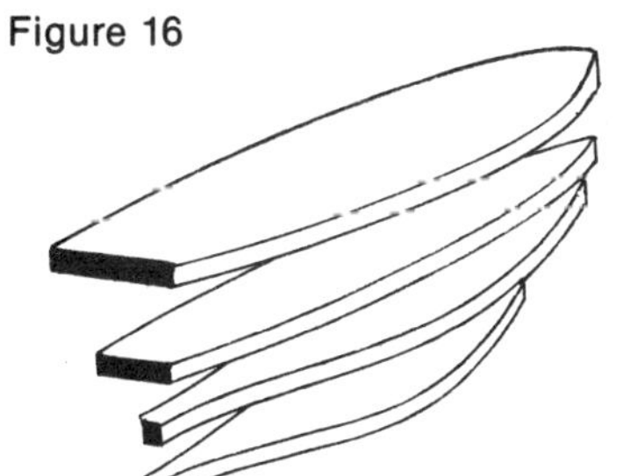

Screw a working base to the keel

Figure 15

THE LAMINATED SOLID HULL

The laminated solid hull is more or less the method employed by naval architects when they prepare builder's "half-models" as a guide for the shipwrights in the yard. In general, the latter are "waterline" models in which each of the board laminates are equal in thickness to the space between waterlines on the drawings. The boards are of contrasting colored woods so that the waterlines would clearly show up in the finished rendition. A "half-model" is simply one side or another of the hull rendered from the center profile out and mounted on a panel as a "bas relief". A half-model makes a very nice piece of decoration in itself and some modellers enjoy carrying a project no further. A beginner may find the creation of a half-model a good first effort. The method is simply to cut out a series of boards in the shape of the waterlines, glue them together, then plane and file the stepped-up composite into smooth curves. The precut waterlines provide a clear guide for the fairing down process. (Figure 16)

THE BUTTOCKS LAMINATE

An alternative to the waterline laminated hull is the buttocks laminate. The principle is the same as for the waterline method except that the boards are precut to the shape of the buttocks and put together vertically rather than horizontally. In this case, each half of the hull is stacked and glued together from the plane of the keel out, then the two halves are glued together. This method has an advantage in holding port and starboard symetry since the pairs of buttocks boards can be matched perfectly before assembly. (Figure 17)

WATERLINE LAMINATE

Figure 16

Boards cut to waterlines

BUTTOCKS LAMINATE

Figure 17

Boards cut to buttocks

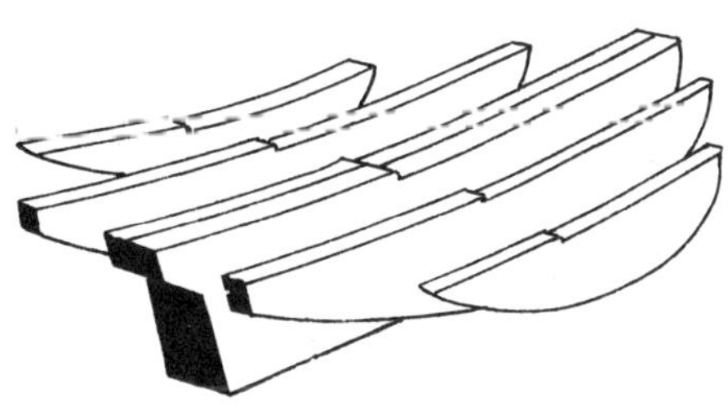

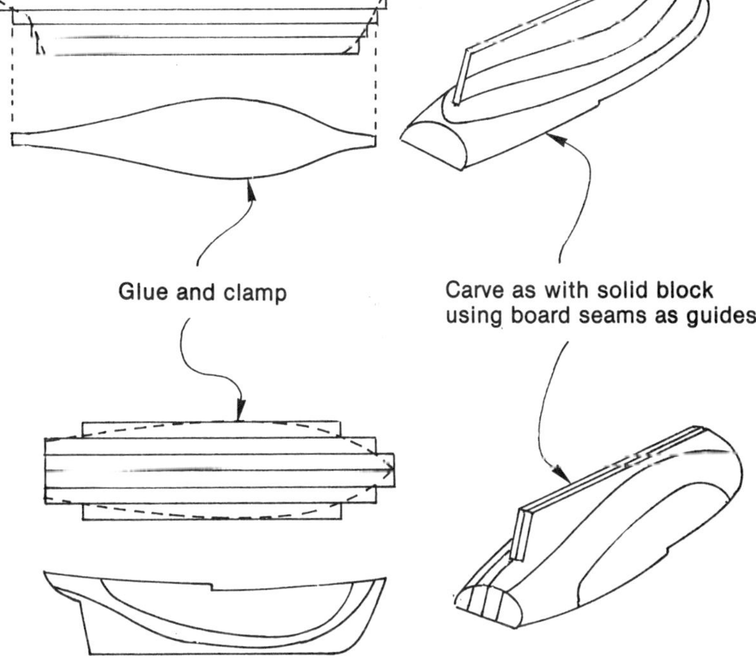

PLANK ON BULKHEAD

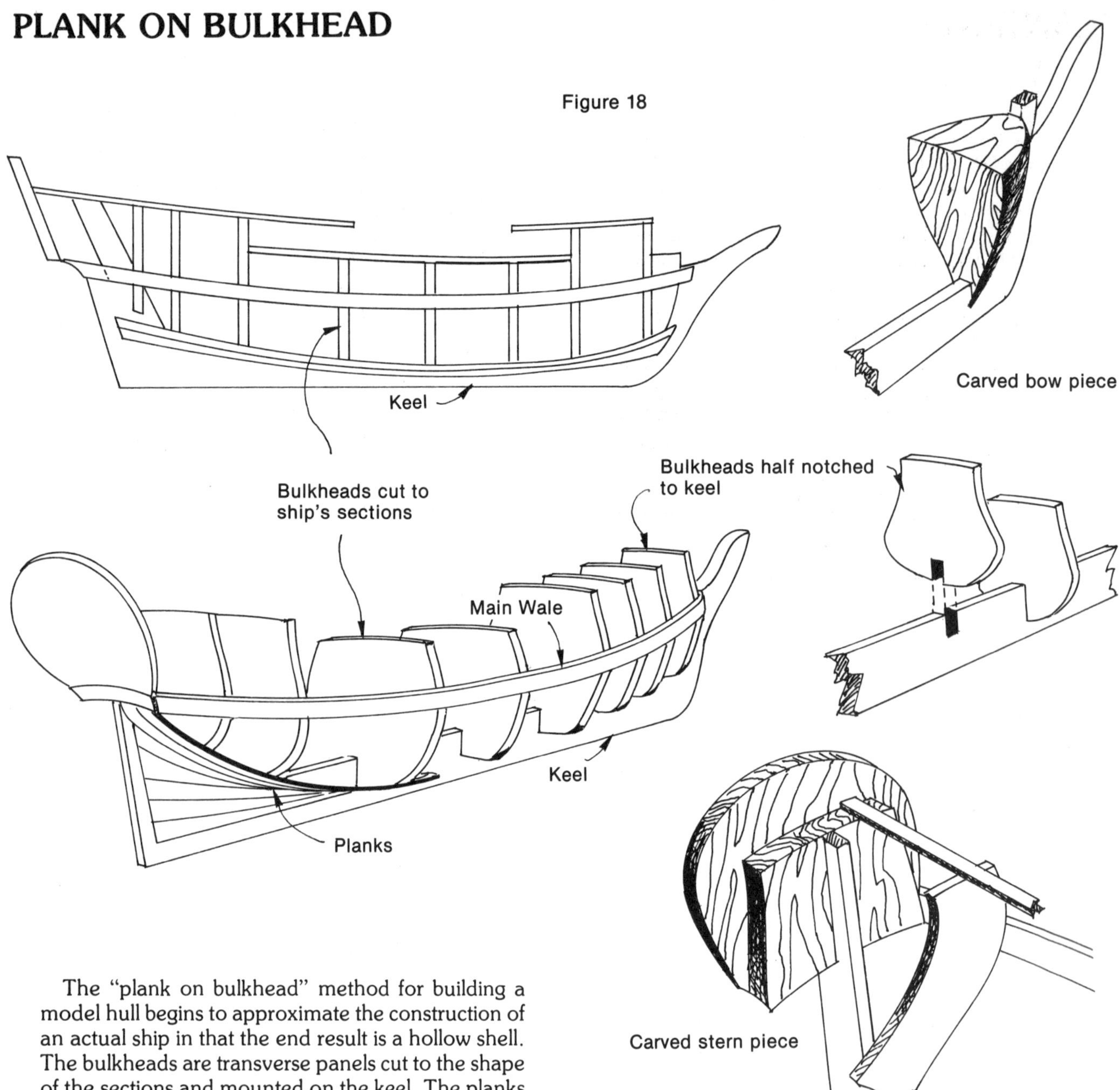

The "plank on bulkhead" method for building a model hull begins to approximate the construction of an actual ship in that the end result is a hollow shell. The bulkheads are transverse panels cut to the shape of the sections and mounted on the keel. The planks are bent and fastened to the edges of the bulkheads in the same manner as the planks on the real ship. The bulkheads do the same job as the real ship's frames. The difference is that a half dozen or so bulkheads serve the modeller for perhaps ten times as many frames of an actual vessel. This detail is ignored in the method because the below decks areas are not seen in the finished product.

The first step in the construction of a plank on bulkhead hull is to cut and assemble the keel, stem and stern posts. Allow enough material on the inboard edge of the keel to permit strong cross notch joints with the bulkheads. Cut out each bulkhead and fit them to the keel with careful attention to their height and general alignment. One way to do this is to cut a waterline template out of stout cardboard and mount it on a couple of blocks so that the template's height matches the height of the line.

Glue a temporary batten across each bulkhead at the same waterline and hang the bulkheads through the template to their place on the keel. Whatever you do in this procedure, be careful of the alignment in all directions. If you're the smallest bit out up and down or side to side, you will have a tough time fairing up the bulkhead edges for the planking.

When the glue has set, fair down the bulkhead edges so the planks will run smoothly. Use a file or long bladed draw knife and imagine that you were shaping the whole surface of the hull. Try to shave down at least a couple of bulkhead edges at once, being careful not to offend the grain too much.

The next step will be the addition of the wales and planks as described on pages 14 and 15.

Plank on bulkhead kits are available.

PLANKING

Simple planking will yield a beautiful hull, which might be painted or finished in natural wood where the scale detail of the various seams and butts of the planks are ignored in favor of a smooth skin of wood. The flow of the ship's planking is suggested by the grain of the wood, and the slight color variations of the various planks. The overall effect is comparable to that of a piece of fine, inlaid furniture.

1) Begin the installation of the sheer plank or wale by cutting the end of a plank so that it makes a neat, clean joint in the groove of the stem, then test to see if the plank can be sprung into position against the bulkheads. If you find the curves are too severe for easy positioning, place the plank on a flat surface and rub it with your knife handle. This rubbing will cause the plank to curl sufficiently to satisfy all but the most extreme bends in the hull.

To get the planks to conform with these very severe bends, you may have to resort to "wet" bending. Wet bending may be accomplished by holding the plank in the spout of a boiling teakettle, or by soaking it in hot water or in household ammonia. Any one of these "wet" treatments will soften the wood fibers and make it possible almost to tie knots with the planks. If you must use wet bending, however, work in the bends over a form or a pattern of nails and let the planks dry completely before installing them on the model, because the planks will expand while wet and shrink again upon drying. If you use steel pins or nails to make a form for such bending, insulate the wet planks from them with plastic wire insulation. Otherwise you stand a chance of the wood being spoiled by rust stains.

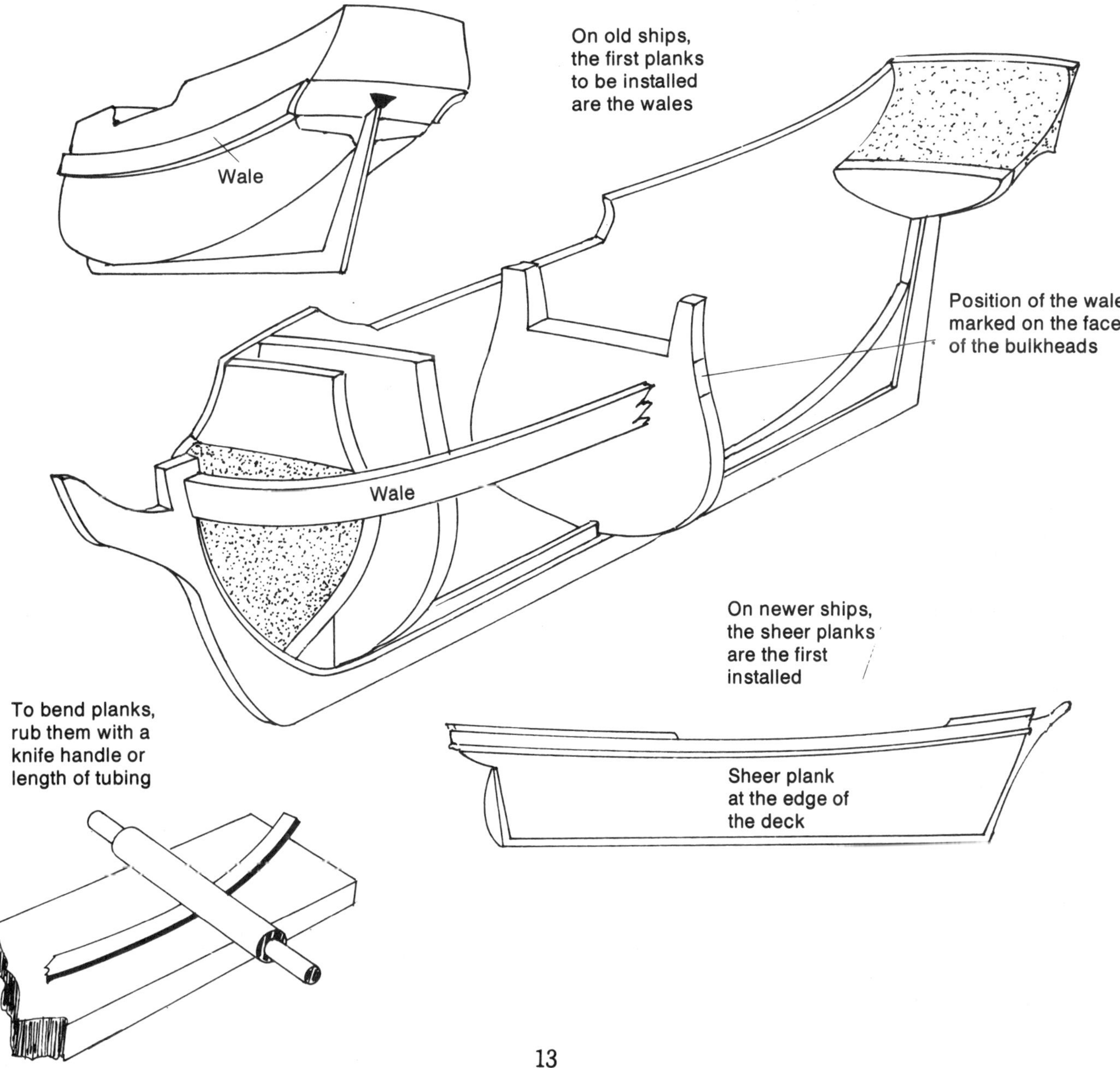

2) Divide each half of the hull into upper and lower portions. The upper portion will consist of the side planking; the lower one, the bottom planking. The line dividing the side and bottom planks will run from the bow at a point around the waterline down under the hull at the middle just where the change from bottom to side is most acute. The shipwrights call this area "the turn of the bilge." From there, the line will run upward again toward the stern, where it will end at the point where the sternpost meets the upper hull. As you proceed with your planking, you will be filling each of these two portions (side and bottom) as if they were separate tasks all together. The side planking will proceed from the sheer plank, or wale, downward; the bottom planking from the keel upward.

3) As you view your model in profile, having marked out the division between the side and bottom, you will see that the upper area is shaped like a quarter moon. It will be clear that to fill the area entirely with planks, you will have either to taper all of the planks as they converge toward the bow, add extra widths of planks midships that are tapered on both ends, or apply a combination of both these expedients. The last will probably prove most satisfactory. So taper the ends of a half dozen or so planks over a length equal to about a third of the length of the model to a width at the end of about a third the width of the stock. Use a small plane or a mill file as shown in the illustration. Fit the tapered ends of the planks to the stem as you did with the sheer plank, working in the bends as required. As you lay each plank, glue it to the one above along its edge as well as to the bulkheads. Try to join the plank edges so that they meet squarely with one another, beveling them particularly where the curves of the ship are most acute.

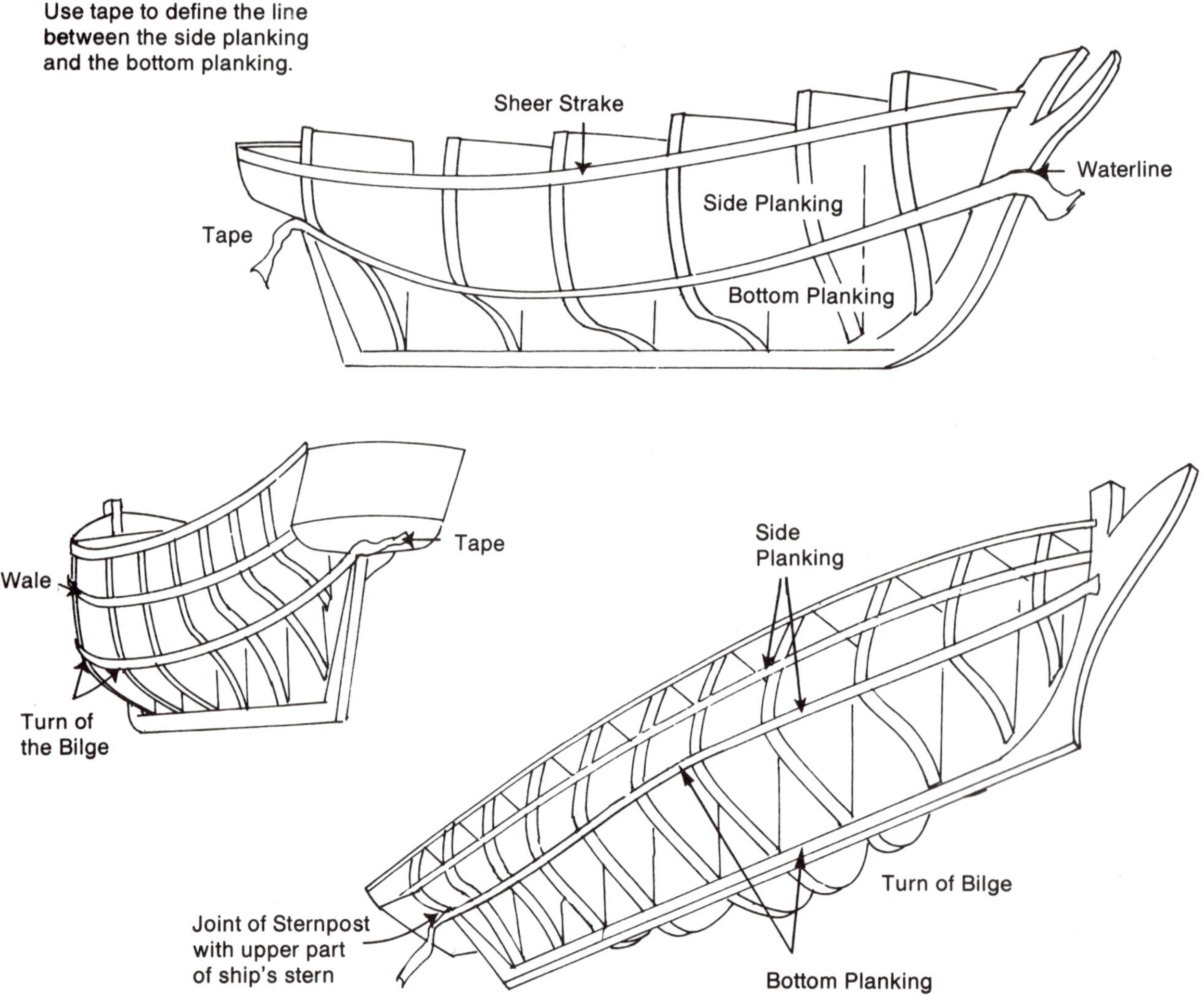

Use glue such as Elmer's Carpenter's Wood Glue, which sets fairly quickly and may be sanded when dry. With such material, the planks may be installed with no other clamps but your fingers to hold them in place until the glue sets. Alternately, you may secure the planks for drying with bent pins or tacks driven into the bulkheads. Try not to penetrate the planks themselves, lest they be split or defaced with unsightly holes.

Install planks on both sides of the ship, alternately checking for symmetry as you go.

4) As you reach the level in your planking where no more planks will fit on the stem within the side planking area, the rest of the side planks will be tapered to points toward the bow. Depending

5) As you view your model from the bottom, with the side planks in place, the shape of the area remaining to be planked on each side will look something like Robin Hood's bow curving from the middle toward the ends where reverse curves fair into the keel. The key characteristic of the bottom planks is that they twist through their lengths, from vertical at the stem and sternpost, to nearly flat at midships. This characteristic, in turn, brings about a second, in that as a pair of planks twist, they naturally tend to fan out from each other.

The side planks as viewed broadside.
The number of planks vary with different ships.

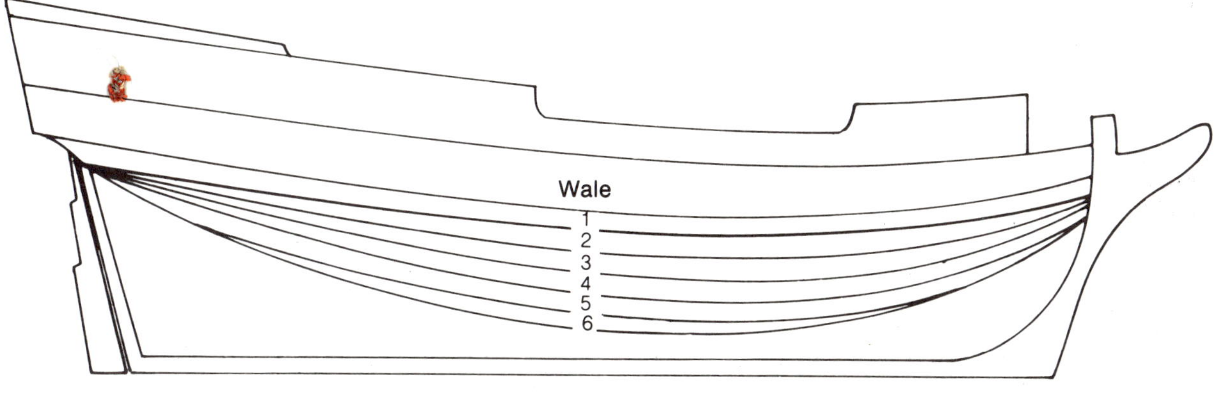

A set of side planks look similar to this
if removed from the hull and laid flat.
Note that planks 5 and 6 taper to points on both ends.
Your model could require more than 2 planks so tapered.

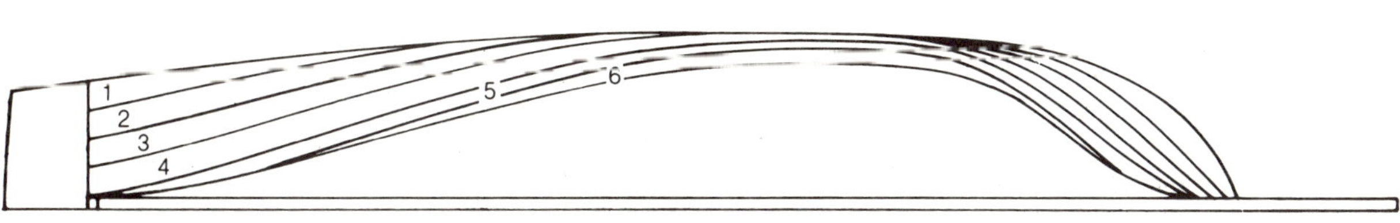

Side planks as viewed from the bottom

6) In laying the first bottom plank next to the keel, shape it so that it tapers from the widest at sternpost and bow, and narrower amidships, as a first step to compensating for the fan effect. Then, as subsequent planks are laid, allow them to fan out on the sternpost. The same effect may also occur at the bow, but as the area to be covered here is smaller than at the stern, you may ignore the fan shapes and fit the planks conventionally.

Triangular-shaped filler planks are made to fit the holes left by the fanned-out full planks at the sternpost.

7) Double-tapered planks may be required to complete the planking at midships similar to that of the side planking.

8) With all the planks in place, sandpaper the hull, removing excess dried glue and sharp corners. During the sanding process, if the edges of the planks have not been joined perfectly, unsightly gaps may show up in the seams. To fill these gaps, glue in slivers of planking material, sand them flush, and the defects will all but disappear.

9) Finish the hull with paint or wood finish as you would a piece of furniture, bearing in mind that a matte or satin finish is to be preferred to a high gloss. The model is now planked and ready for the construction of the decks and upper works.

Bottom planks as viewed from the side.
The number of planks will vary with different ships.

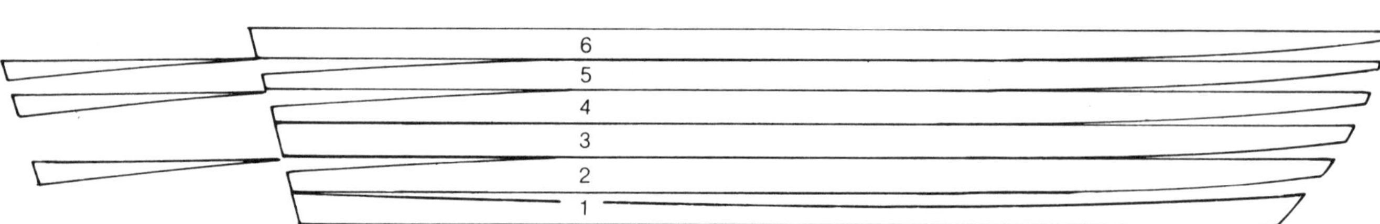

A set of bottom planks look similar to this
if removed and laid flat. Note triangular fillers
near the stern, and the reverse taper of plank 1.

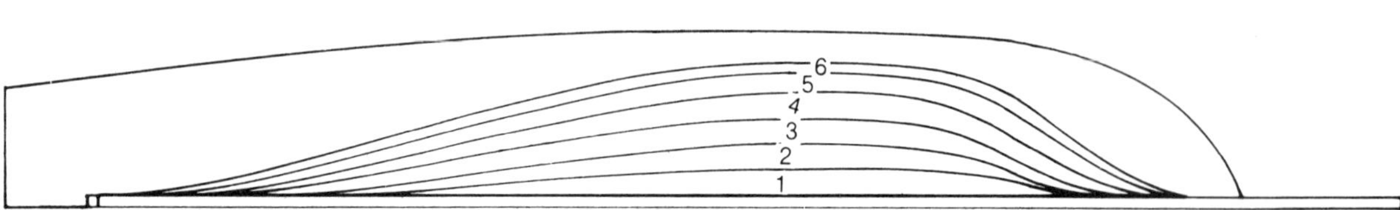

Bottom planks as viewed from the bottom.

DECKS

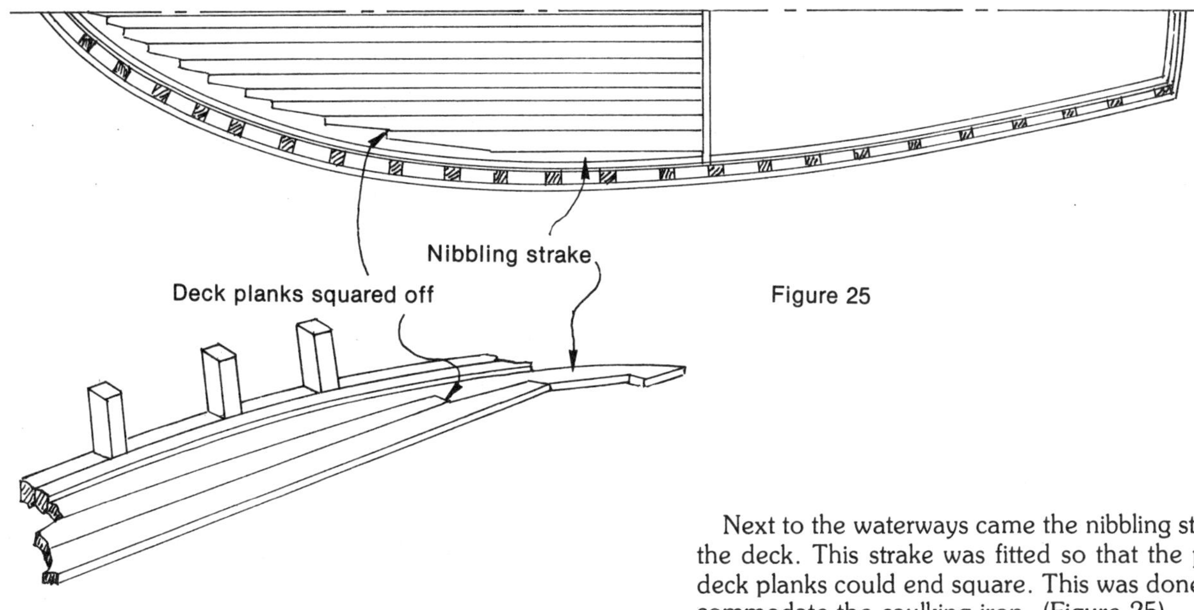

Next to the waterways came the nibbling strake of the deck. This strake was fitted so that the parallel deck planks could end square. This was done to accommodate the caulking iron. (Figure 25)

Model decks may be planked a board at a time or put down in a single piece scored to show the plank seams. Deck planks were from 4" to 6" wide.

Your model may require that one or several partial decks be built up over the main deck. If this is the case, cut deck beams to the proper camber and fit them to strips equivalent to a real ship's "clamp strakes". A clamp strake is the first ceiling strake under a deck beam.

Scuppers are slots, or holes, in the bulwarks at the level of the deck so that water can run overboard. Sometimes scuppers had hinged covers on the outboard side. Inside water pressure opened them; gravity closed them.

DECK CAMBER   Figure 26

Arc of Circle

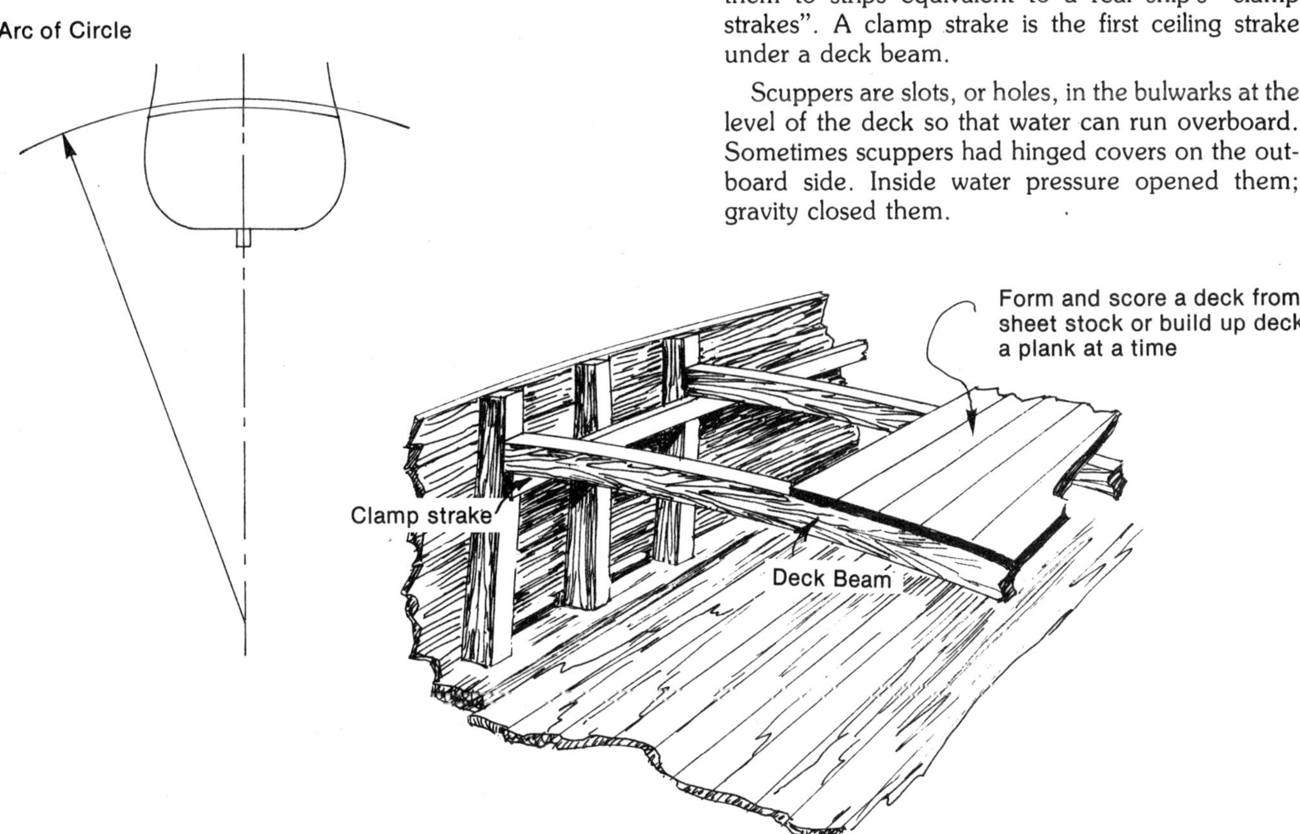

STERN AND QUARTER SECTIONS

Ships of the seventeenth and eighteenth centuries had stern and quarter galleries. These galleries were essentially platforms built out from the ship proper as extensions of the deck. Initially, the galleries had only a rail around them and were roofed by the deck above. But gradually they evolved into narrow little cabins planked up and fitted with windows.

The quarter galleries served primarily as the officers' latrines. The stern galleries served as an observation platform and a place where the ship's V.I.P.'s could take the air in privacy and shelter.

The period of these ships was the period of high baroque art in Europe, when sculpture and painting twisted and writhed with soaring figures, winged cupids and all sorts of elaborate decoration. The enthusiasm for this art carried over into the ships, and perhaps nowhere was it more apparent than in the stern and quarter galleries. These parts were carved all over with figures, mythical beasts, coats of arms, and stylized foliage. (Figure 28)

The taffrail was the panel of the stern above the water. It earned its name from the Dutch *tafreel;* literally a panel picture which indeed it was, as taffrail carvings and decoration were often the most elaborate of all.

About 1610 William Pett, a famous English shipwright introduced the "round tuck" stern. In this construction planks ended on a horizontal transom beam set like the top of a "T" on top of the stern post. In earlier, "square tuck" construction, the planks ended on the after most frame of the ship. (Figure 27).

Modified round tuck stern construction has remained the standard to the present day.

SQUARE TUCK STERN
standard before 1610

Figure 27

ROUND TUCK STERN
standard after 1610

Figure 28

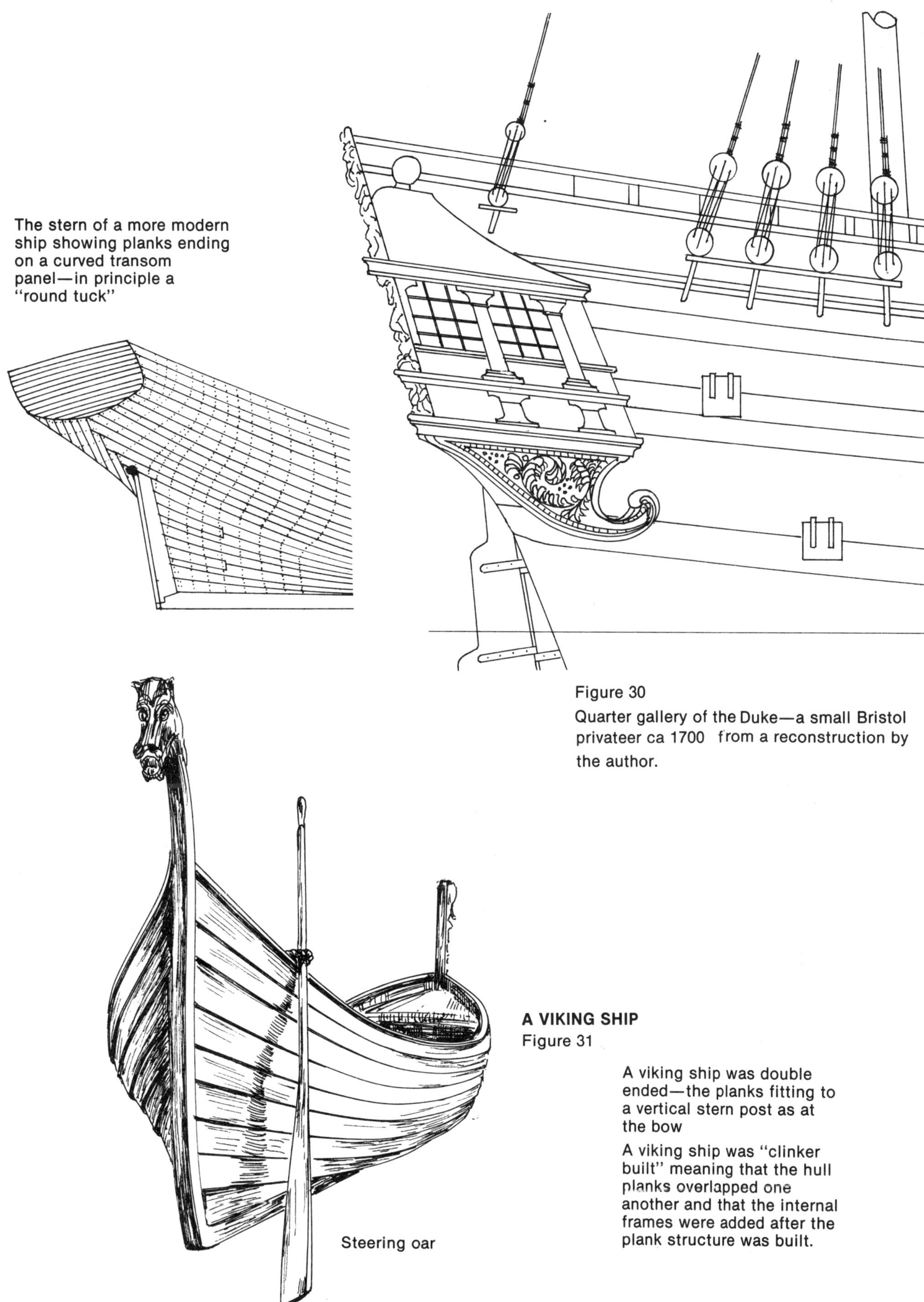

The stern of a more modern ship showing planks ending on a curved transom panel—in principle a "round tuck"

Figure 30
Quarter gallery of the Duke—a small Bristol privateer ca 1700 from a reconstruction by the author.

A VIKING SHIP
Figure 31

A viking ship was double ended—the planks fitting to a vertical stern post as at the bow

A viking ship was "clinker built" meaning that the hull planks overlapped one another and that the internal frames were added after the plank structure was built.

Steering oar

BOW AND HEAD SECTIONS

The bows of a ship built before 1820 or so were characterized by the head rails and the long reverse curve of the stem ending in the figure head.

The head rails served as the crew's latrine facilities. There were always three of them. From top to bottom, they were the hair rail (so called because it ended in the "hair" of the figurehead); the middle rail and the lower rail. The lower rail came down to the level of the main deck and the head gratings. In top view the head rails ran straight out to a point on the forepeak; in side view they made sweeping parabolic curves down from under the catheads and up to the forepeak.

Below the head rails (and not to be confused with them) are the cheek knees of the head. The cheek knees continue the line of the main wale sweeping up in a strong curve to the forepeak. Through the cheek knees inboard are the hawse pipes for the anchor cable. In top view the cheek knees appear as curves connecting the hull and the stem. They form lateral reinforcement for the stem.

After 1835 more or less, bows grew longer and more tapered. Head rails disappeared and trail boards took up the job of the cheek knees. Trail boards were often decorated with scroll carvings and the ship's name.

The bows of ships varied from very elaborate to very simple. The simplest bow was the billet head.

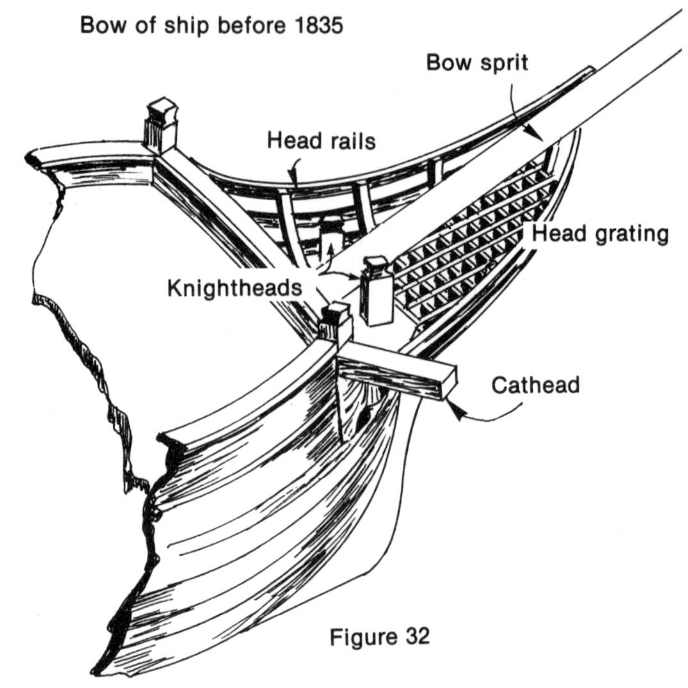

Figure 32

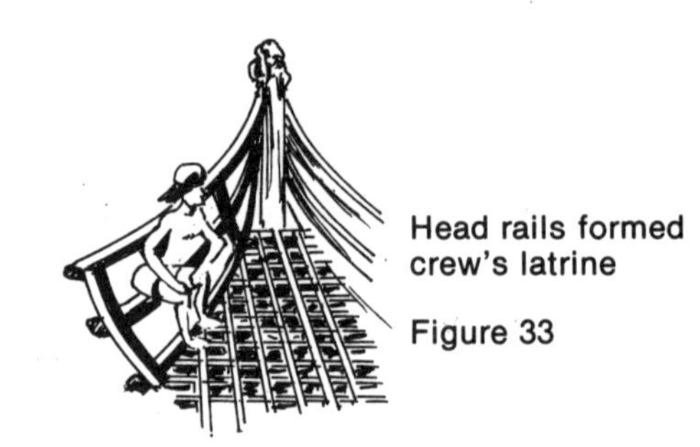

Figure 33

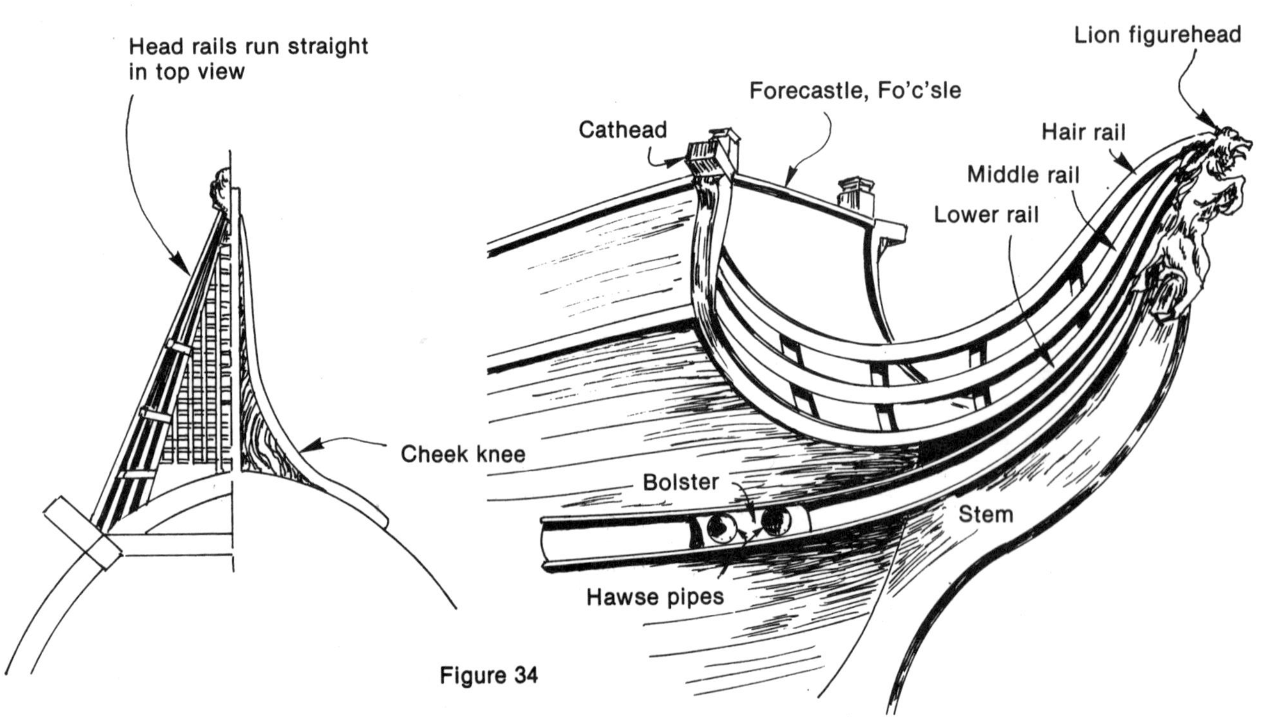

Figure 34

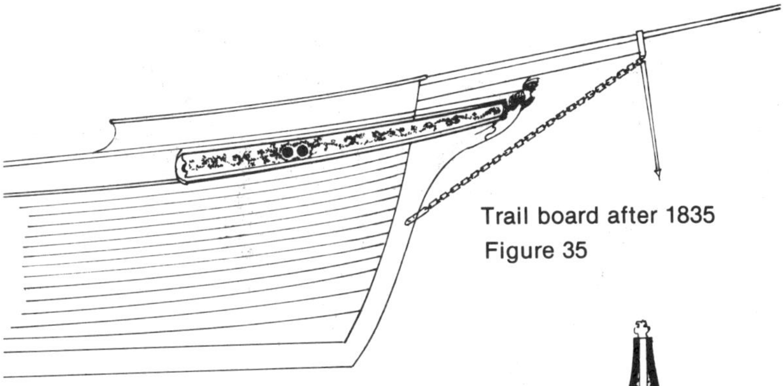

Trail board after 1835
Figure 35

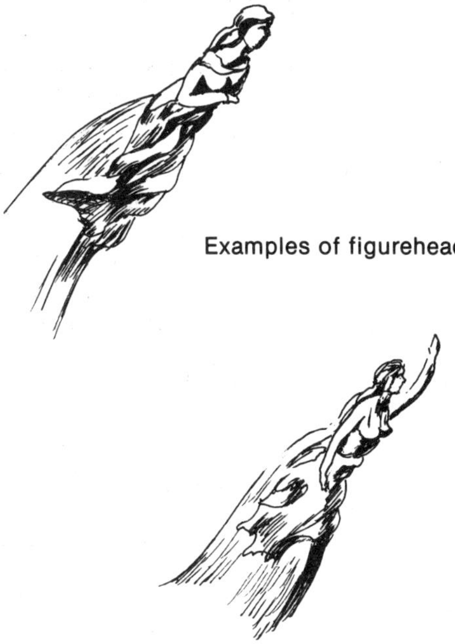

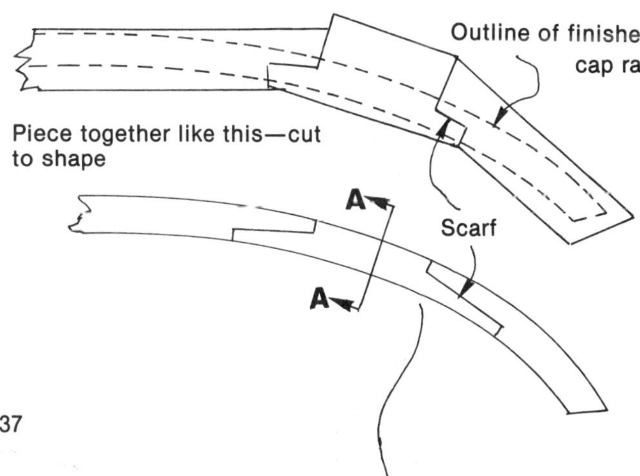

Examples of figureheads

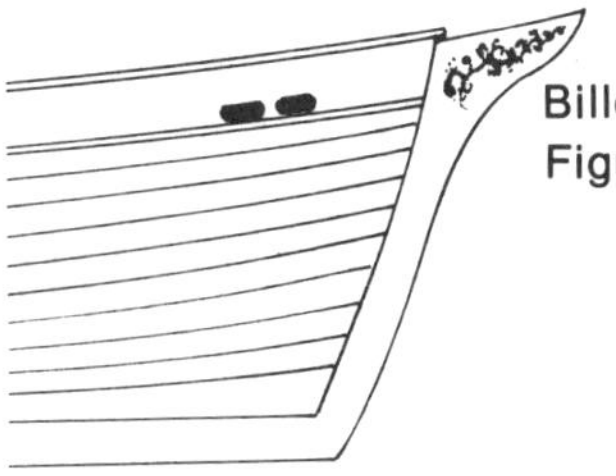

Billet head
Figure 36

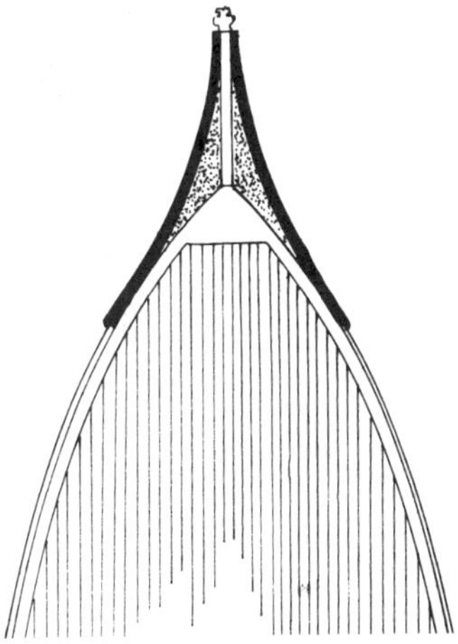

Trailboard and cheek
after 1835

CAP RAILS

Piece together the cap rails as shown in figure 37. Take special care in this detail because for some reason carelessly built cap rails stand out on a model more than other things.

Representative cross
sections of cap rails

A A

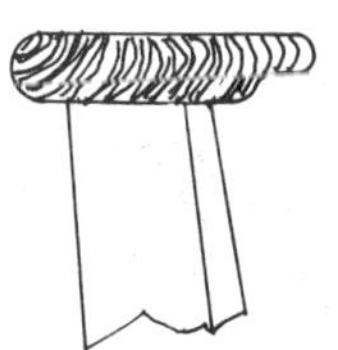

Piece together like this—cut
to shape

Figure 37

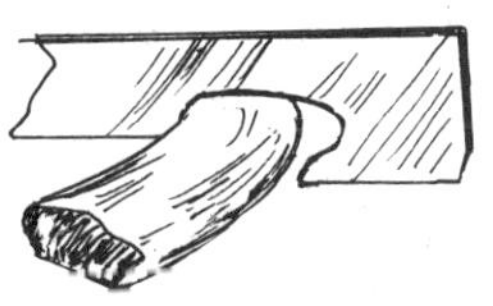

Shape a piece of hacksaw
blade to cross section of cap
rail. Use it to scrape the rail
to shape

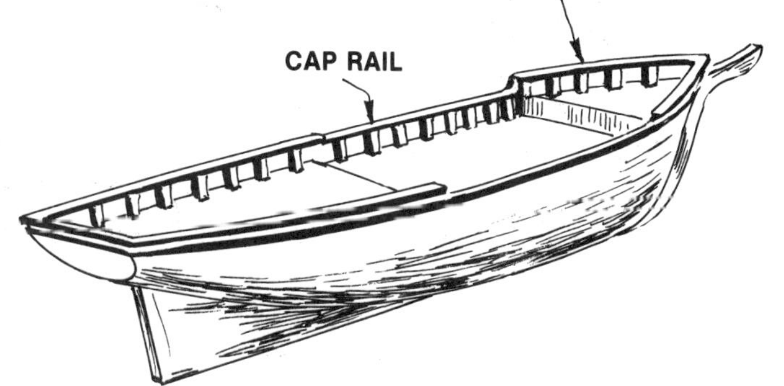

FURNITURE

The equipment that is fastened down to the deck of your ship is loosely termed "furniture" or deck furniture.

A few examples of deck furniture are shown here but each ship had its own unique set.

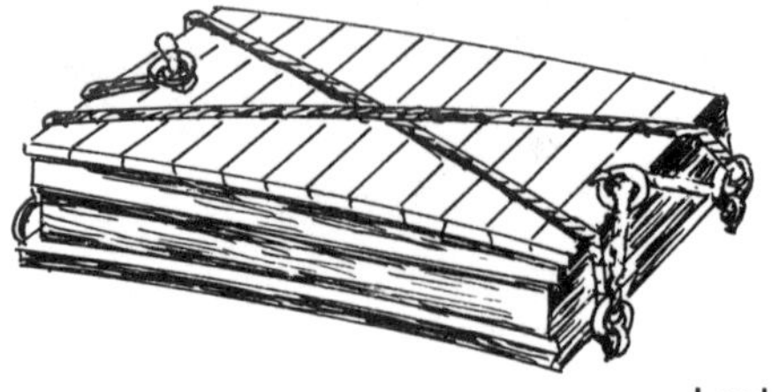

Hatch cover for merchantman

Lashed down

HATCHES
Figure 38

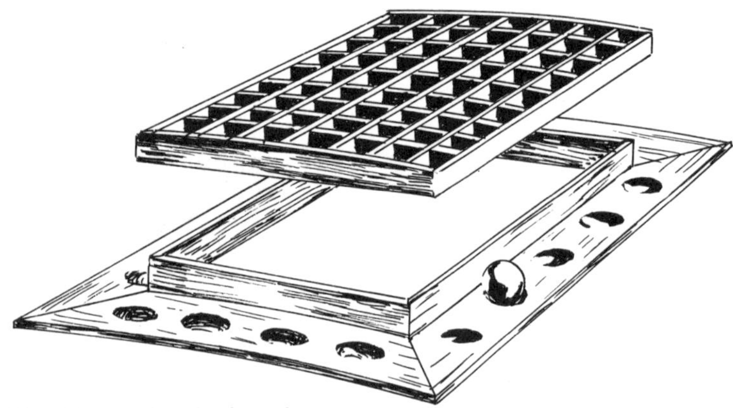

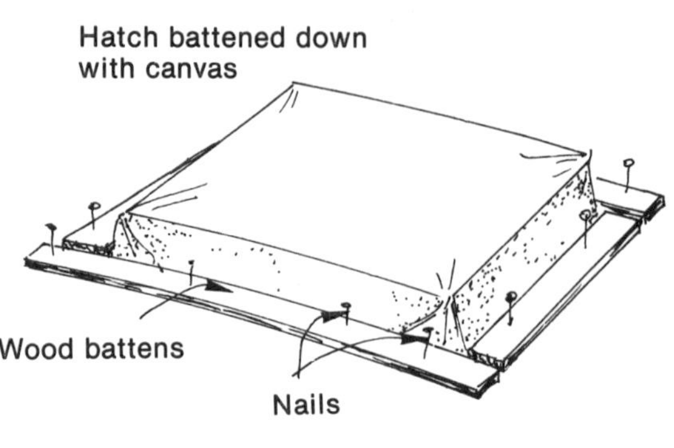

Hatch battened down with canvas

Wood battens

Nails

Warship hatches had grating covers for ventilation

Gratings are available in pre-cut components ready to assemble

Another way hatch covers were fastened down

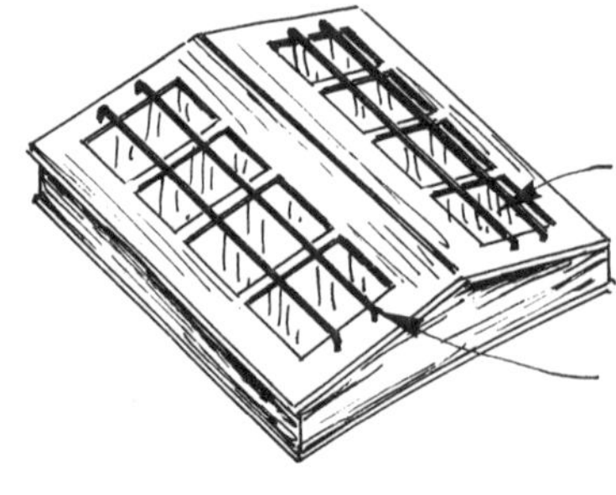

Skylight   Figure 39
Use plastic or glass for lights

Wire protectors

MAKE A GRATING LIKE THIS
Figure 40

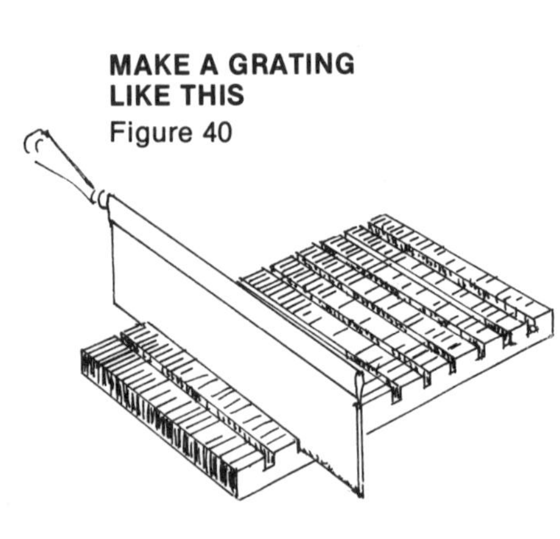

1. Clamp together strip stock
2. Saw half through

3. Interlock strips, glue

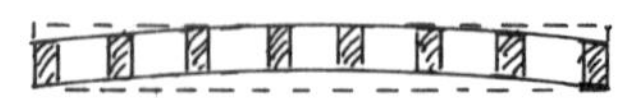

4. Shape to deck camber

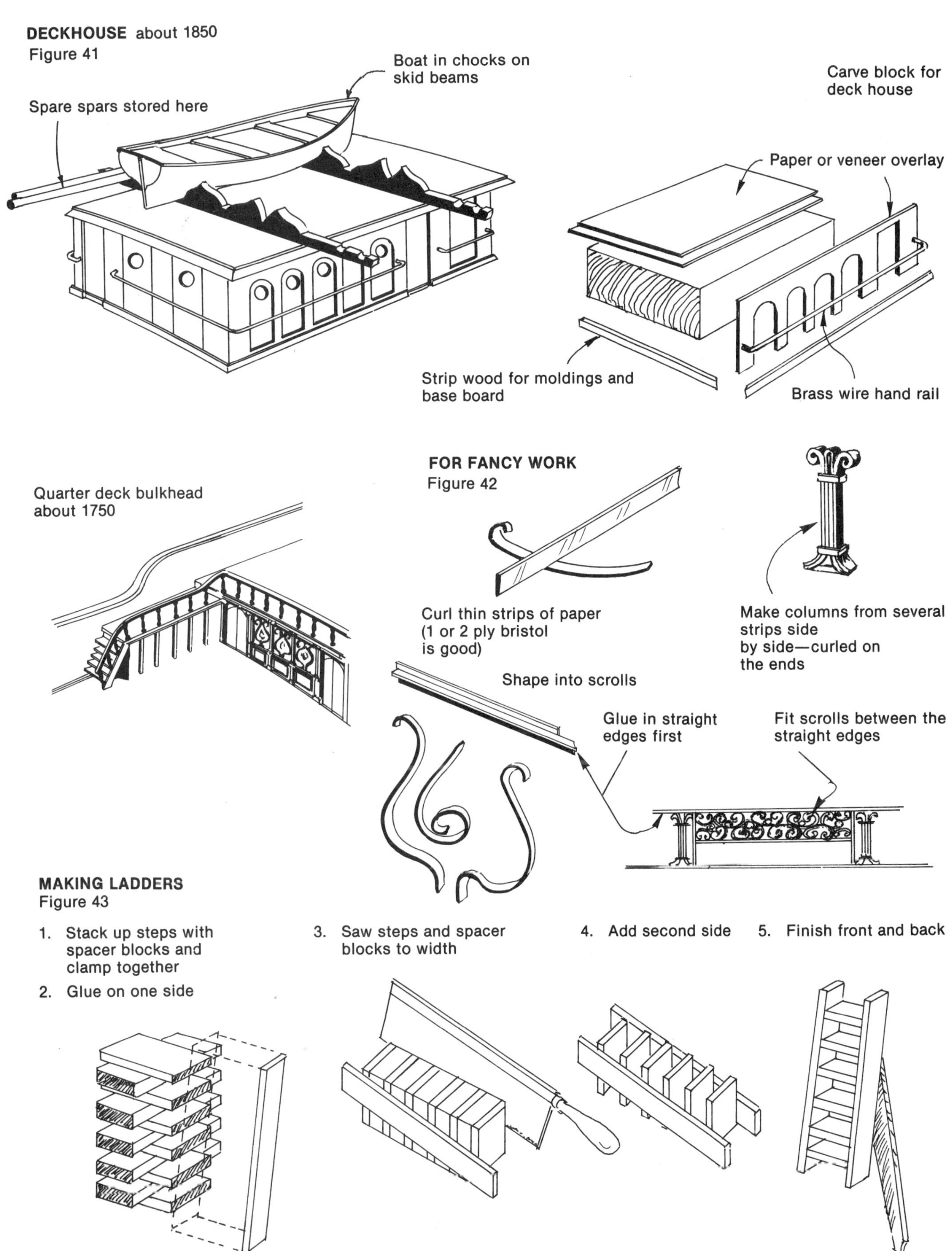

DECKHOUSE about 1850
Figure 41
Spare spars stored here
Boat in chocks on skid beams
Carve block for deck house
Paper or veneer overlay
Strip wood for moldings and base board
Brass wire hand rail
Quarter deck bulkhead about 1750
FOR FANCY WORK
Figure 42
Curl thin strips of paper (1 or 2 ply bristol is good)
Shape into scrolls
Glue in straight edges first
Make columns from several strips side by side—curled on the ends
Fit scrolls between the straight edges
MAKING LADDERS
Figure 43
1. Stack up steps with spacer blocks and clamp together
2. Glue on one side
3. Saw steps and spacer blocks to width
4. Add second side
5. Finish front and back
Ladders are available as prefabricated fittings

GEAR FOR HANDLING LINE

A sailing ship was equipped with an assortment of gear for hauling and fastening lines.

An early windlass was a horizontal wooden barrel mounted between uprights fastened to the deck. It was equipped with a ratchet that kept it from running backward under the strain of a line; holes in the barrel took the handles. Whelps fed the turns of the line toward the outer ends of the barrel.

A more modern windlass substitutes a rocking arm handle for the earlier pole handles.

A capstan was a vertical barrel mounted between two or more decks. Holes in the cap took the turning bars, and whelps fed the turns of the line upward.

Fife rails were mounted near the foot of the masts and were variously fitted with holes for belaying pins, sheaves, cleats, and other equipment. Frequently fife rails were mounted with the fore or main bitts as our illustration shows.

Early ships and smaller ships of a later age had only a bitts at the fore and main mast.

Pin rails were mounted all along the bulwarks of many merchant ships while naval ships used the fife rails for most of their lines. Naval ships needed the bulwarks clear for guns.

Kevels (cavils) were used to tie off especially heavy lines such as the top sail halliards, main sheet or main tack.

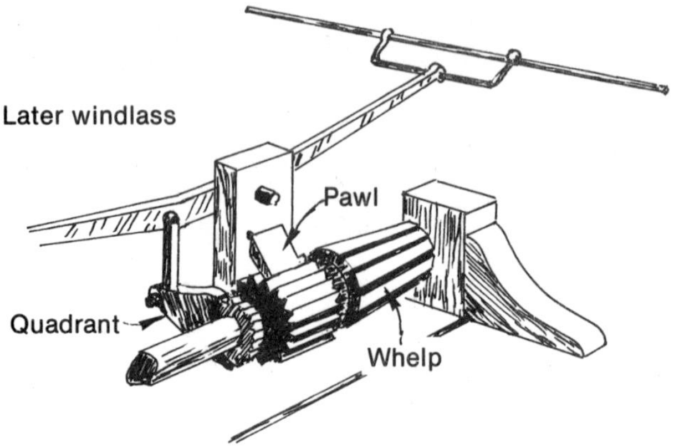

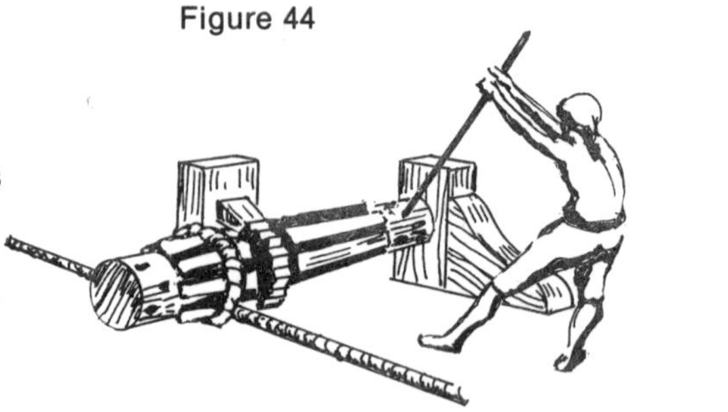

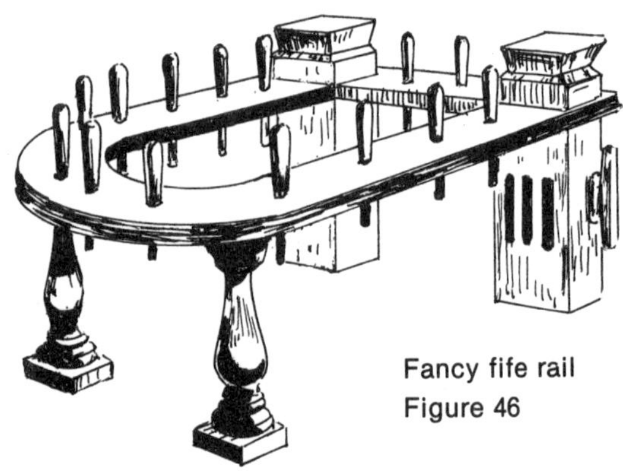

Later windlass

Figure 44

Early windlass

Capstan
Figure 45

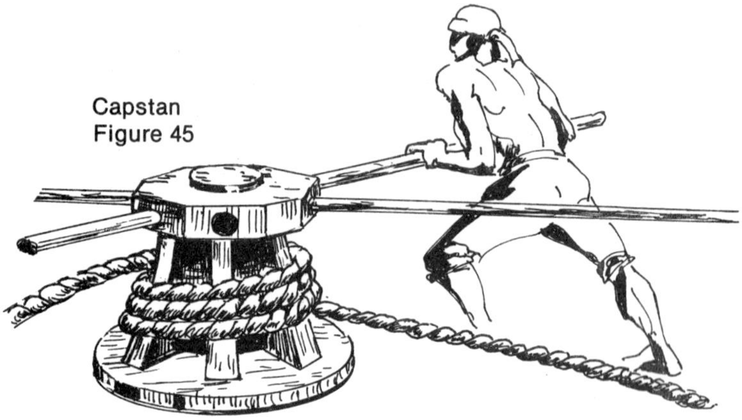

Fancy fife rail
Figure 46

Knight
Figure 47

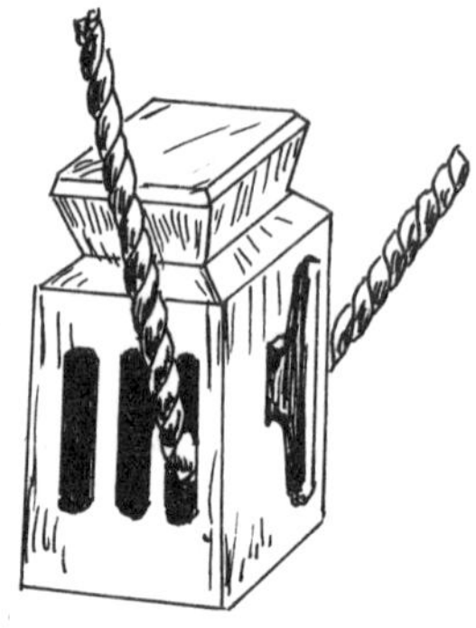

KEVEL (CAVIL) Figure 49

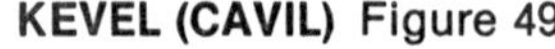

Bitts Figure 48

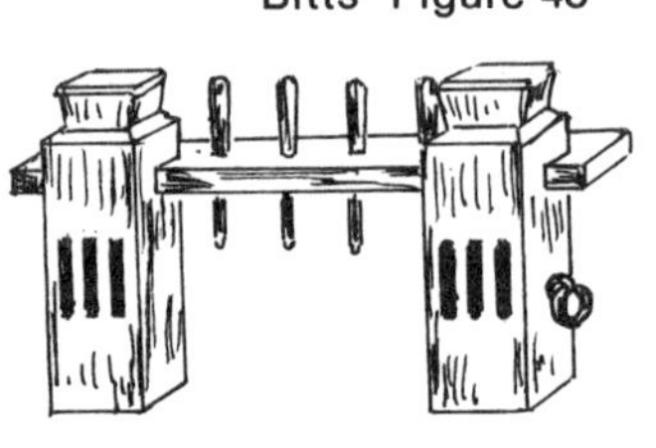

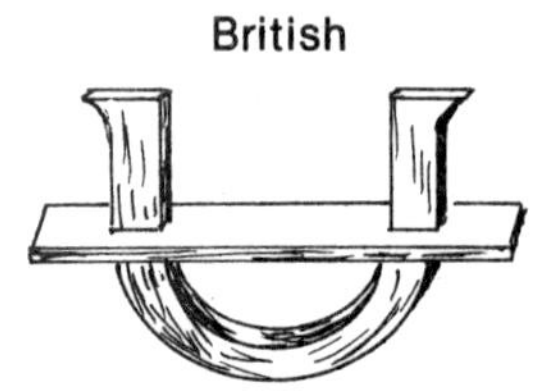

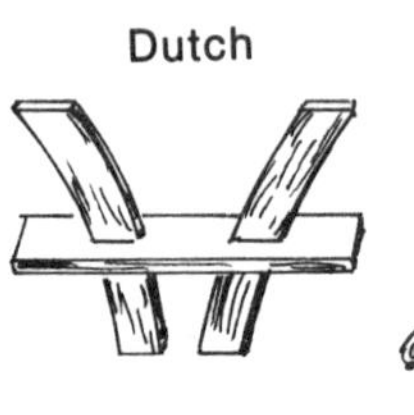

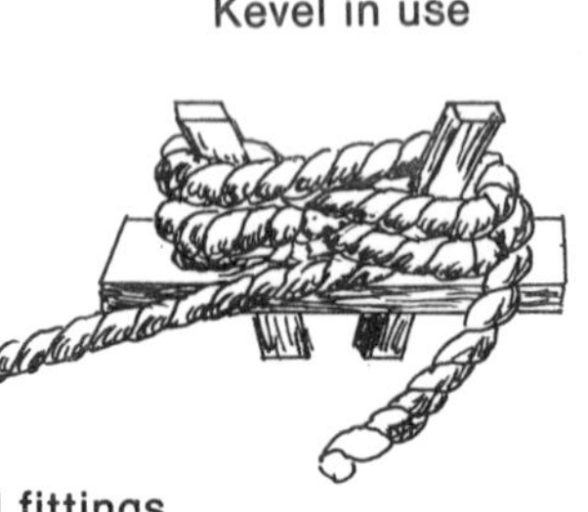

Many of the parts on this page are available as prefabricated fittings.

STEERING GEAR

The key element of a ship's steering gear is her rudder. A rudder works by slowing down the flow of water on one side of the ship. The effect is to turn the bow of the ship toward the side where the water has been slowed.

The rudder in most ships is turned to either side with a tiller, an arm attached to its upper end or stock. The steerage of smaller ships and boats often consists of no more than the rudder and its tiller.

In larger ships additional gear was used to turn the proportionately heavier and more remote tiller/rudder apparatus. The sum of all this gear is called a ship's helm and the man who steers the ship is the helmsman.

Up to about 1700, a ship's tiller was worked by a "whipstaff". The lower end of the whipstaff was loosely attached to the inboard end of a long tiller. The staff then went up through the deck where it was pivoted to a beam or block. The helmsman swung the whipstaff from side to operate the tiller (Figure 52).

The whipstaff would not permit the rudder to be turned very far so the helms of these old ships were not too efficient. In fact, the sailors of the time depended more on their head sails for maneuvering than they did on their rudder. The rudder did more in holding a course than it did in changing course.

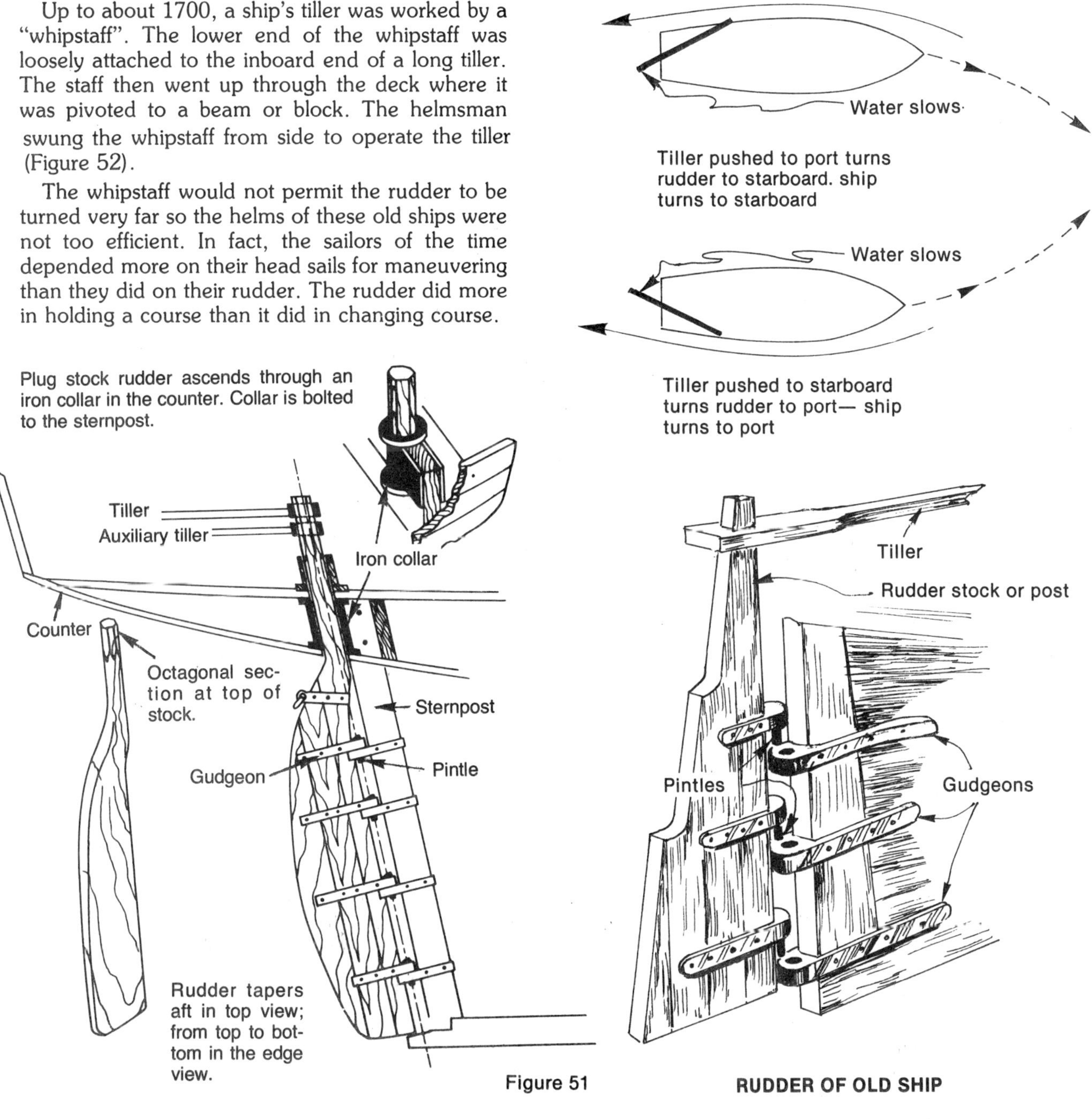

STEERING GEAR (cont.)

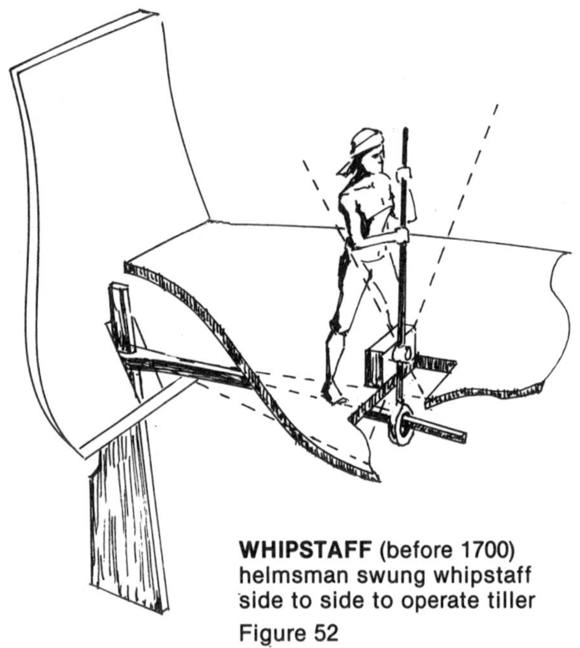

WHIPSTAFF (before 1700)
helmsman swung whipstaff
side to side to operate tiller

Figure 52

After 1700 steering wheels began to replace the whipstaff so that by the middle of the century the latter were obsolete. Steering wheels were rigged above and below decks as shown in figures 53 and 54.

This arrangement, allowing for variations in size and a switch to chain cordage in later years, remained essentially unchanged from 1700 to about 1850. Thereafter, rudder machinery increased in complexity as ships grew to large modern proportions. The tiller was replaced by a quadrant and the helm became power driven for example.

The terminology surrounding a ship's helm often refers to the wind direction. For example, a captain wishing to bring his ship about orders "make ready to come about". When the lines are properly manned the mate reports, "Ready to come about, sir." The captain at the crucial moment then says, "Ready about!" This alerts the crew. Then follows "helm alee!" On this command the helmsman pushes the tiller as far to the lee side of the ship as possible, so that the rudder turns to windward and the ship heads up into the wind. (See figure 8, page 7). "Lee helm" on a ship is considered a safe helm because it means that the ship has a natural tendency to head up into the wind, (a safe situation) and the helmsman must keep pressure on the tiller to keep the ship "off". The opposite is a "weather helm" where the ship tends always to steer downwind and it becomes hard work to get her to head up.

**STEERING WHEEL
RIGGED TO TILLER
ABOVE DECK**

Figure 53

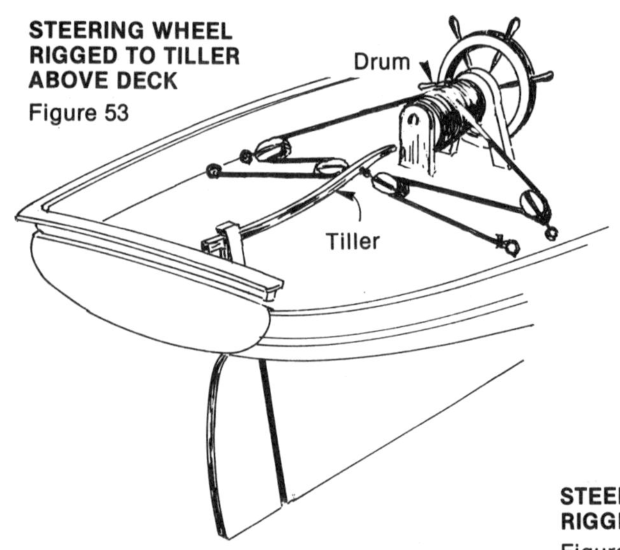

**STEERING WHEEL
RIGGED BELOW DECKS**

Figure 54

Single part tackles on small
ships—multi part tackles on
larger ships

Sheaves

Tiller

The number of spokes in a
steering wheel is determined
by its size and a man's reach

Wheel boxes enclosed drum
and other steering gear

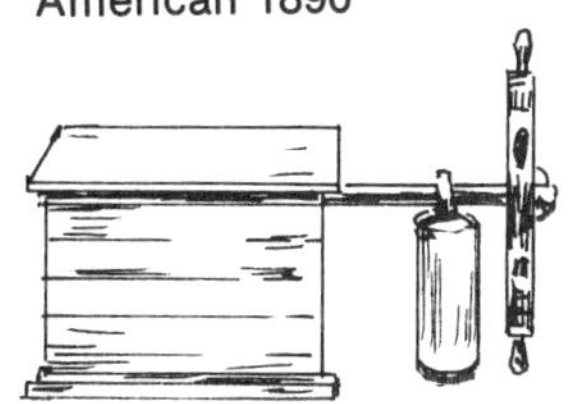

Steering wheels are available as prefabricated fittings.

WHEEL STANCHIONS
Figure 56

After stanchion (aft of
the drum)

FITTING A RUDDER
Figure 57

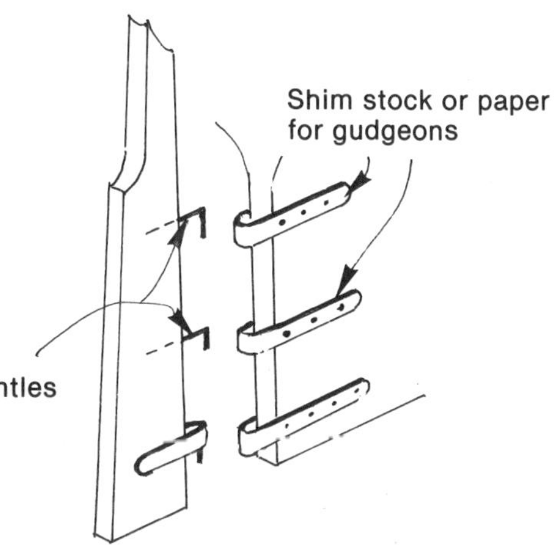

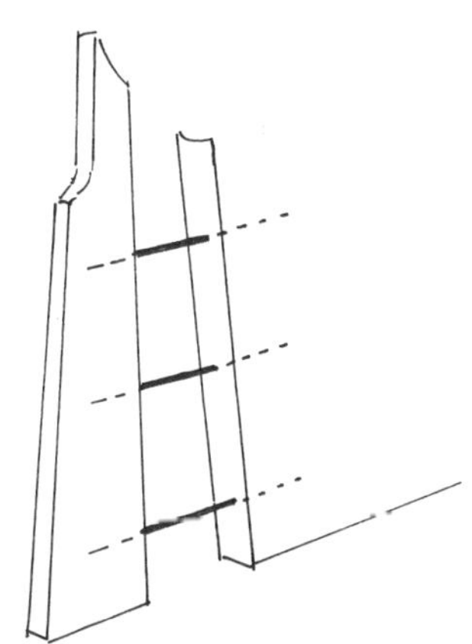

GROUND TACKLE

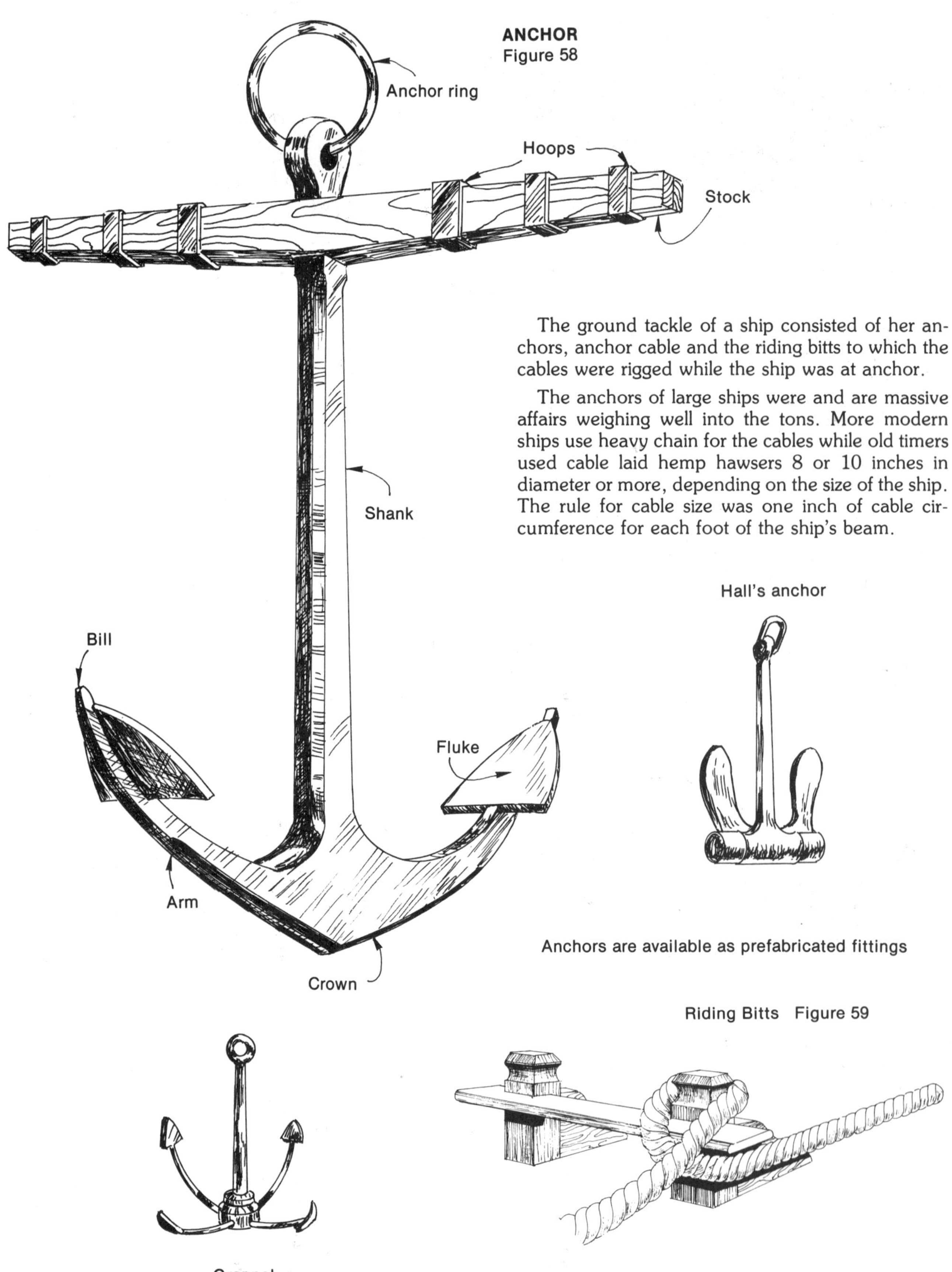

The ground tackle of a ship consisted of her anchors, anchor cable and the riding bitts to which the cables were rigged while the ship was at anchor.

The anchors of large ships were and are massive affairs weighing well into the tons. More modern ships use heavy chain for the cables while old timers used cable laid hemp hawsers 8 or 10 inches in diameter or more, depending on the size of the ship. The rule for cable size was one inch of cable circumference for each foot of the ship's beam.

Anchors are available as prefabricated fittings

CATHEADS AND BILLBOARDS

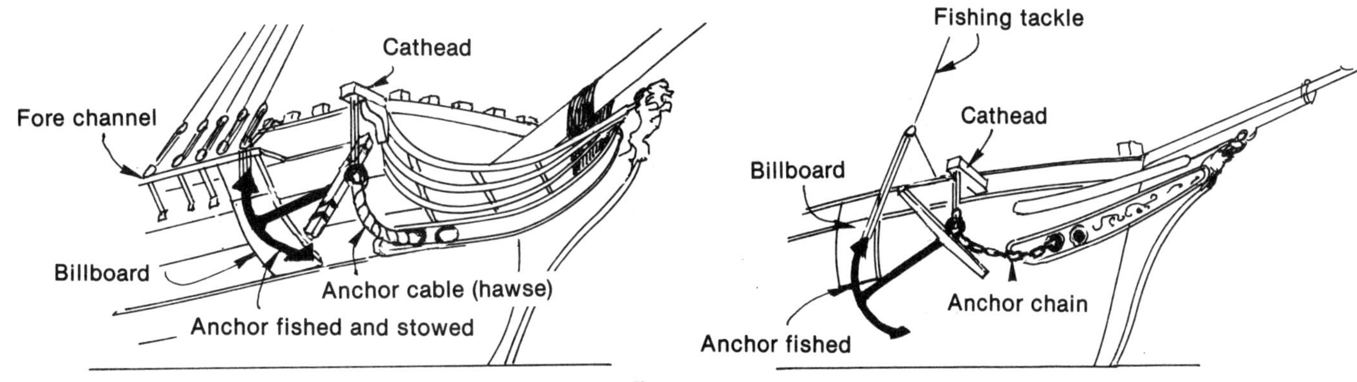

Figure 60

Old timers carried their anchors outboard, "fished" up against the bows. The ring end of the anchor was hoisted clear of the water through tackle rove into the catheads. The bill end was hoisted up with tackles rigged high on the mast or topsail yard. Once fished, the anchor was lashed up tight to the fore chains or to the fore rail. The shipside where the bill of the anchor rode was protected by billboards.

Later, ships carried their anchors inboard lashed down to the fore deck. The catheads and billboards still functioned while the anchor was in process of being dropped or weighed.

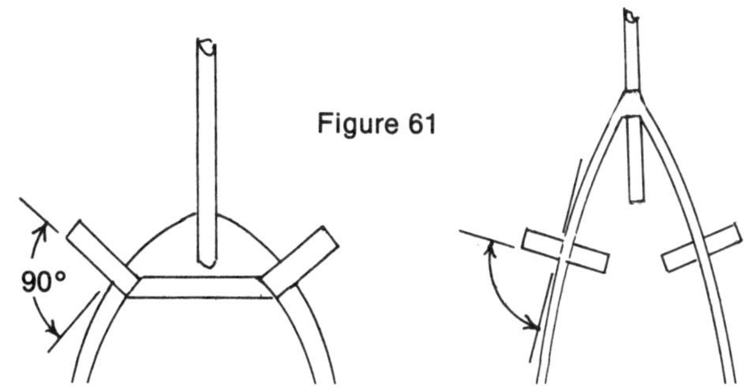

Catheads were fitted
90 degrees to the ship side

WEIGHING ANCHOR
Figure 62

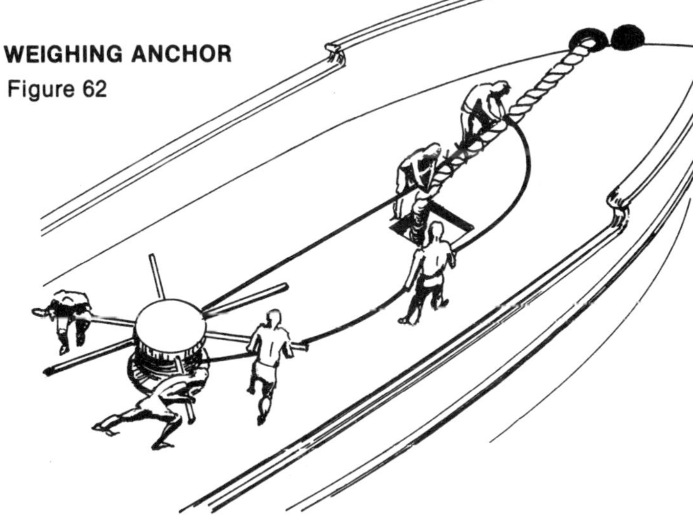

Seamen weighing anchor
with messenger line

Weighing anchor (hauling it in) was a heavy job. The hauling was done indirectly with a messenger line, a long loop running from the cable to the capstan and back again. The messenger line was tied and untied to the cable as the cable came aboard and was fed down through a hatch to the hawse locker below (Figure 62).

MAKING AN ANCHOR Figure 63

1. Cut shank and arms from sheet metal

2. 'Super' glue or solder flukes

3. Fit stock

4. Add hoops—paper or shim stock

GUNS AND GUNPORTS

Between 1500 and 1835 more or less the great oceans were battlegrounds. The seafaring nations of Europe were at war for the trade of the world, not least of which was that of the "New World"—the Americas. Therefore, all ships whether merchantmen or naval vessels went to sea prepared to fight. Guns were the major weapons.

The gun deck of a ship in those days in combat was a horror.

The deck would be crowded with perhaps a hundred men or more. The only light and ventilation was that which crept through the deck gratings and gun ports. Lanterns or candles were lethal in the atmosphere of wood and gun powder. It was dark, wet, and stinking.

With the order to fire, the guns would go off one after another in a series of mind numbing bangs made worse by the restricted space. If they were all fired at once the combined recoils would tear out the side of the ship. They had no recoil mechanisms, so the guns would buck off the deck at each firing and slam back into their breechings. The smoke of burnt powder and steam from cooling water would choke the atmosphere.

Let a man touch a gun chase in the pandemonium and his hand would fry. Let him misjudge his place in the thundering gloom and he would be crushed by a rearing gun carriage.

Add to this enemy fire, splinters flying like buckshot, the moans of wounded, disoriented crew mates, and blood, fear and pain. Such was the glory of naval warfare that one can feel fortunate to have missed.

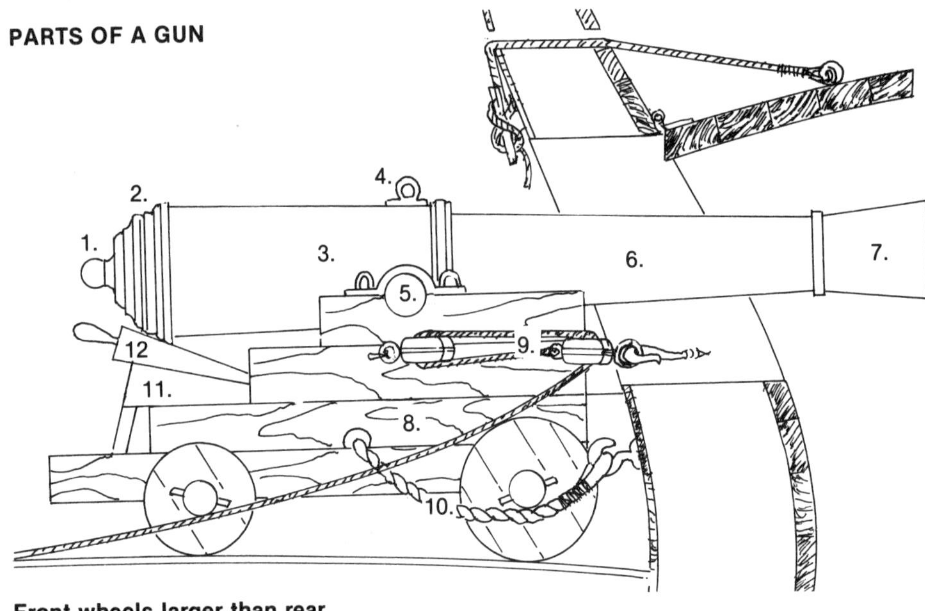

Front wheels larger than rear makes gun level on cambered deck

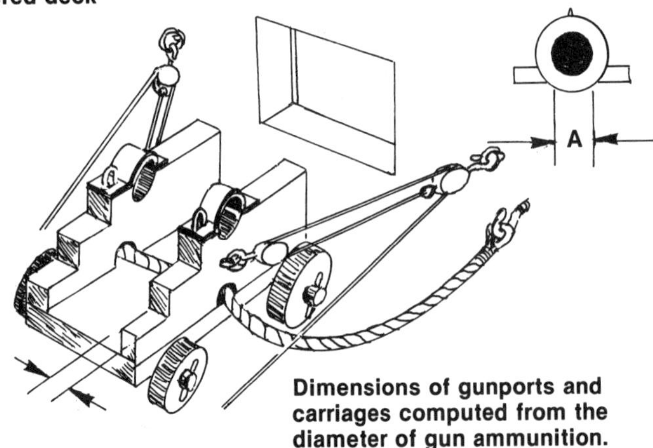

Dimensions of gunports and carriages computed from the diameter of gun ammunition.

1. CASCABEL
handle for aiming or lifting gun

2. TOUCH HOLE
hole takes priming power—match touched here fires gun

3. REINFORCE
multiple in some guns, e.g. first reinforce, second reinforce, etc.

4. DOLPHIN
lifting ring

5. TRUNNION
bar that supports gun in carriage

6. CHASE
main barrel of the gun

7. MUZZLE SWELL

8. GUN CARRIAGE

9. TRAIN TACKLE
hauls gun out and helps in aiming

10. BREECHING
controls recoil

11. BED
adjusts gun elevation— works with quoin

12. QUOIN
adjusts gun elevation— works with bed

Guns and gun carriages are available as prefabricated fittings

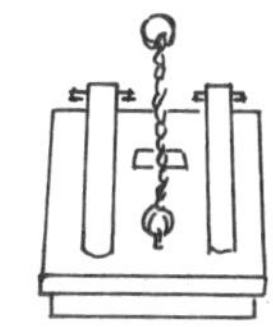
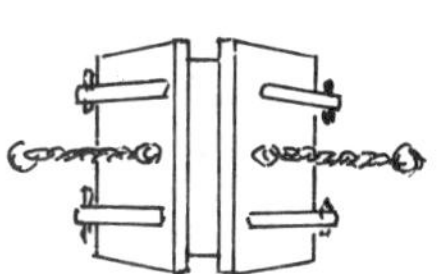
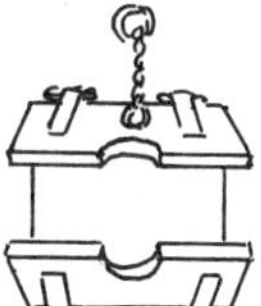
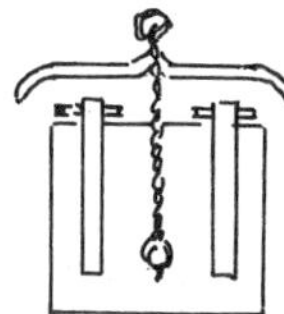

Gunport covers varied in design

Plot line of gun ports per dimensions below

Dimensions of gunports are computed from the diameter of the gun ammunition

a	equals	shot dia. x 25
b	equals	shot dia. x 6:5
c	equals	shot dia. x 6
d	equals	shot dia. x 3.5

The shot diameter for a...

1 pounder	equals	1.9"
6 pounder	equals	3.5"
12 pounder	equals	4.4"
18 pounder	equals	5.0"
24 pounder	equals	5.5"
36 pounder	equals	6.3"

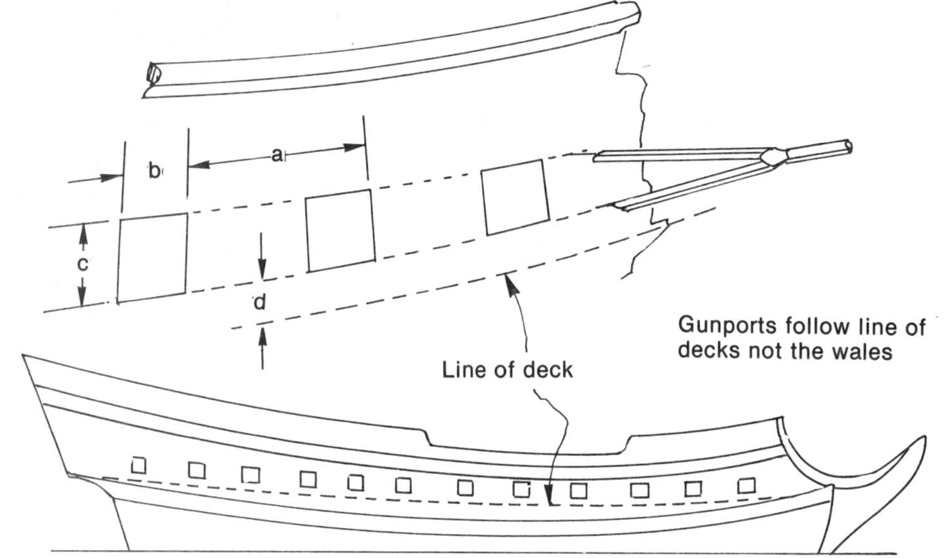

LANTERNS AND LIGHTS

Light was at a premium on old ships since its only source was candles and lanterns and these implied open flames. Fire even more than the sea was the seaman's greatest fear. His ship was made of wood.

In the 17th century large stern lanterns with horn lenses served to keep ship's in visual contact with one another at night.

Kerosene lanterns came into use in the 19th century and the practice of port and starboard running lights was adopted.

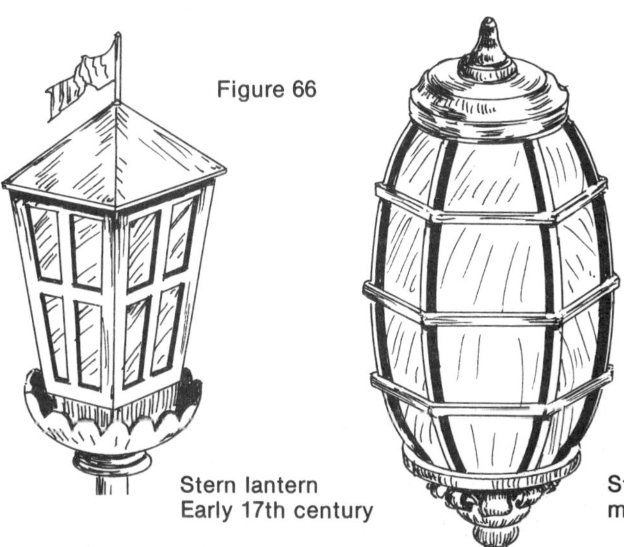

Figure 66

Stern lantern
Early 17th century

Stern lantern
mid 17th century

Lanterns and lights are available as prefabricated fittings

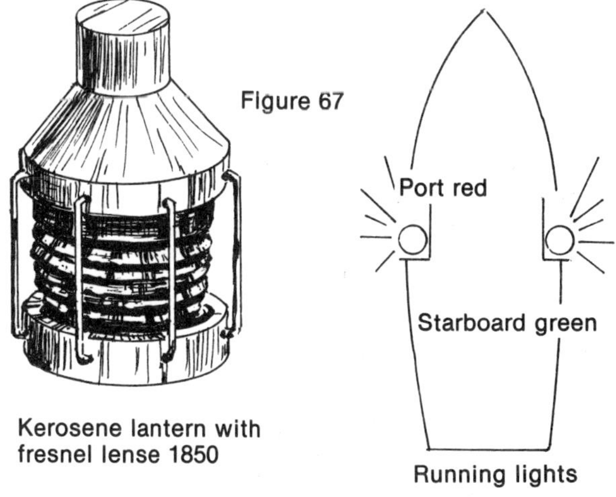

Kerosene lantern with fresnel lense 1850

Starboard lantern board

BOATS

The most famous confusion of the landsman in nautical lore is the difference between a boat and a ship.

One goes to sea aboard a ship, not a boat. Boats are small service vessels for a ship. Classed among boats are the captain's gig, the fisherman's dory, a ship's long boat, the whalerman's whale boat, and life boats.

Before the day of motors, most boats were rowboats, sometimes fitted up for a mast and sail. As a rule, boats were open, that is deckless. Oarsmen sat on plank thwarts, one or two men to a thwart with their backs to the bow. The gunwales (the upper rails of a boat) had thole pins fitted into them as the lever points for the oars. Aft a bos'un manned a tiller.

Small ships sometimes towed their boats astern with a painter line, though this was frequently a problem in heavy seas. Most often, as soon as a ship was off soundings, her boats were shipped and lashed to the deck upside down. In other cases, boats were stowed right side up in chocks on deck or on skid beams mounted athwartships on top of a deck house.

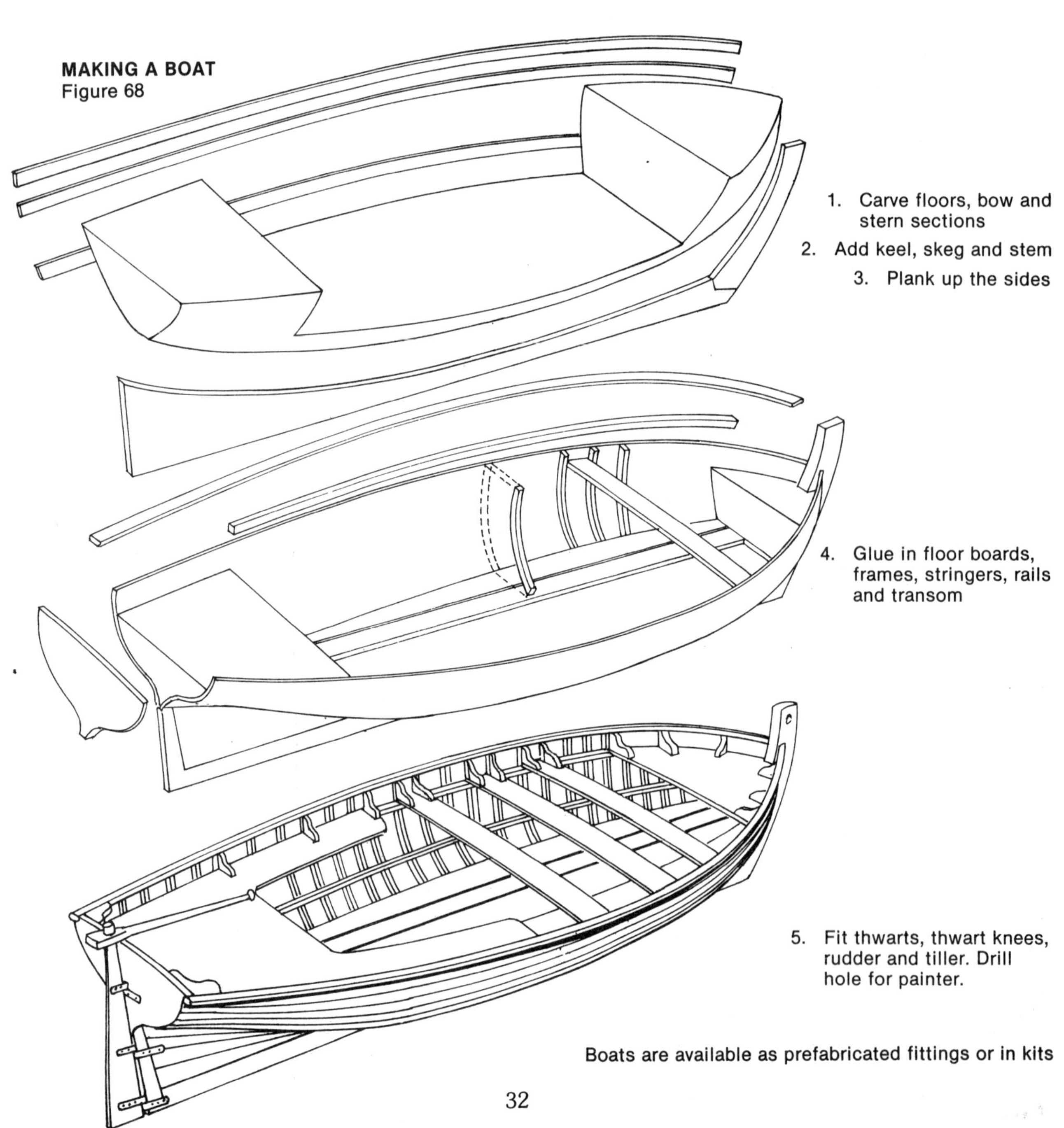

Boats are available as prefabricated fittings or in kits

DAVITS

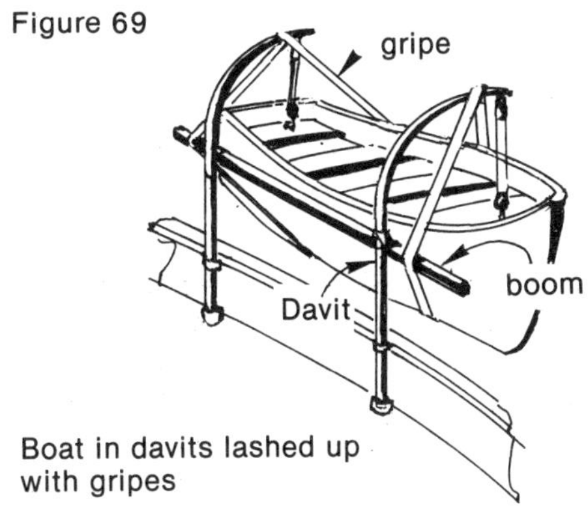

Boat in davits lashed up with gripes

Davits are the special cranes rigged to lower or ship boats. Old ships used straight wooden davits, while after 1850 or so curved iron davits became the rule. Many davits were semi permanent fixtures. That is they could be taken down when not in use and stowed in the hold. Often, however, it was convenient to simply leave the davits rigged up and tied off at the shipside or stern.

Some ships, whalers for example, carried boats outboard in permanent, rigidly fixed davits. Stern davits in the case of the whalers were stout beams bolted to the after rails or the deck.

Later, ships carried life boats pre-rigged to davits along the ship sides.

Boats carried in the davits were lashed up with gripes to keep them from banging around.

The more modern curved iron davits were designed to pivot around so that the suspended boat could be swung in and out over the rail with some ease.

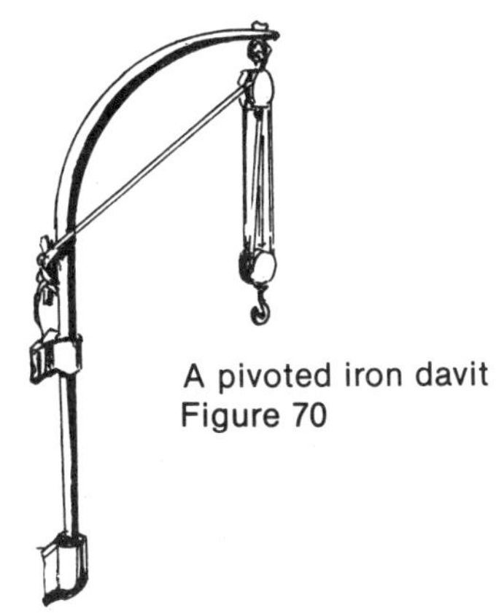

A pivoted iron davit
Figure 70

Lowering a life boat with pivoted, iron davits

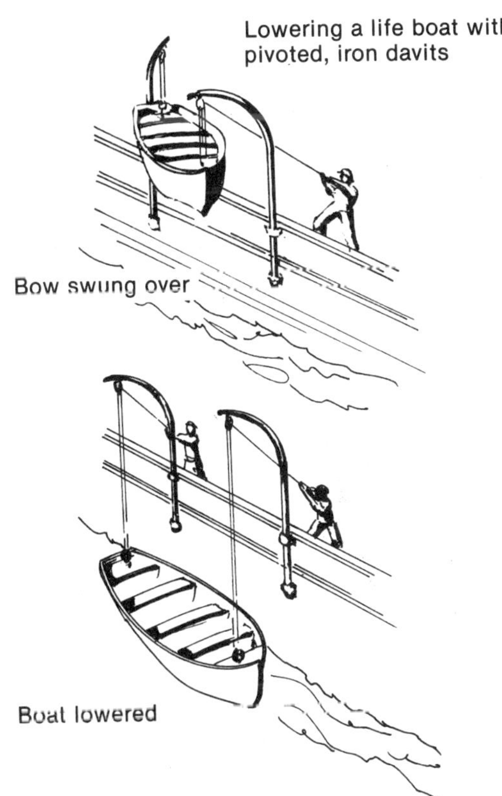

Bow swung over

Boat lowered

Davits are available as prefabricated fittings.

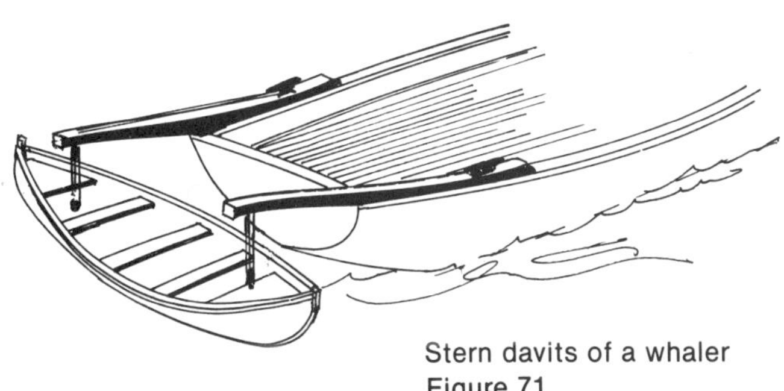

Stern davits of a whaler
Figure 71

Figure 72   18th century man o'war had davits in her mizzen channels

MASTS

Spar is the general term for the various poles that support a ship's sails. Masts are the vertical spars that rise off the deck. Most of the other spars are attached to the masts.

Masts (except in the case of small vessels and most modern yachts) were built up one on top of the other in a structural system that remained essentially unchanged from Columbus' Day to the end of the classic days of sail.

The lower mast rose to the trestle trees and cross trees on which was mounted the top, a platform for various gear and on which the crew worked. The trestle trees supported the heel of the topmast which rose up through the cap of the lower mast. For a few feet the topmast overlapped the lower mast. This overlapped section was called the doublings.

Above the topmast was rigged the topgallant mast in much the same way. Next higher came the royal mast, the sky sail mast and finally on some of the giants of the late 19th century, the moon sail mast.

The top gallant, royal, skysail and moonsail masts were most commonly a single pole rising from the top mast doublings, though sometimes they were built up like the lower masts.

The lower masts of a vessel went down through the decks often to the top of the keel or keelson, sometimes to a lower deck beam. The foot of the mast was mounted in a base structure called the mast step, while the hole in the deck was stoutly reinforced all around with partners. A mast coat was fitted around the mast at the uppermost deck to make the juncture water tight.

Some masts were built of a single tree trunk. Others were pieced together from cut lumber. The latter were nailed and bolted together along their length then reinforced with iron hoops or heavy lashings called wooldings.

Sometimes single trunk masts also were reinforced with wooldings to keep them from splitting.

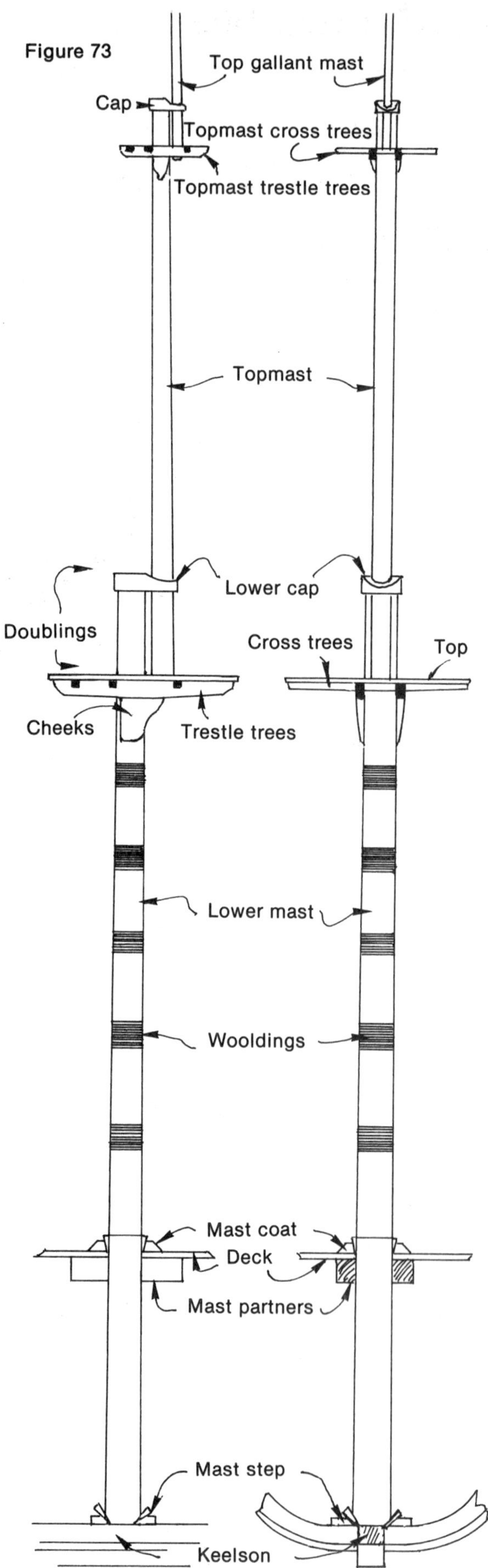

MAST STRUCTURES Figure 74

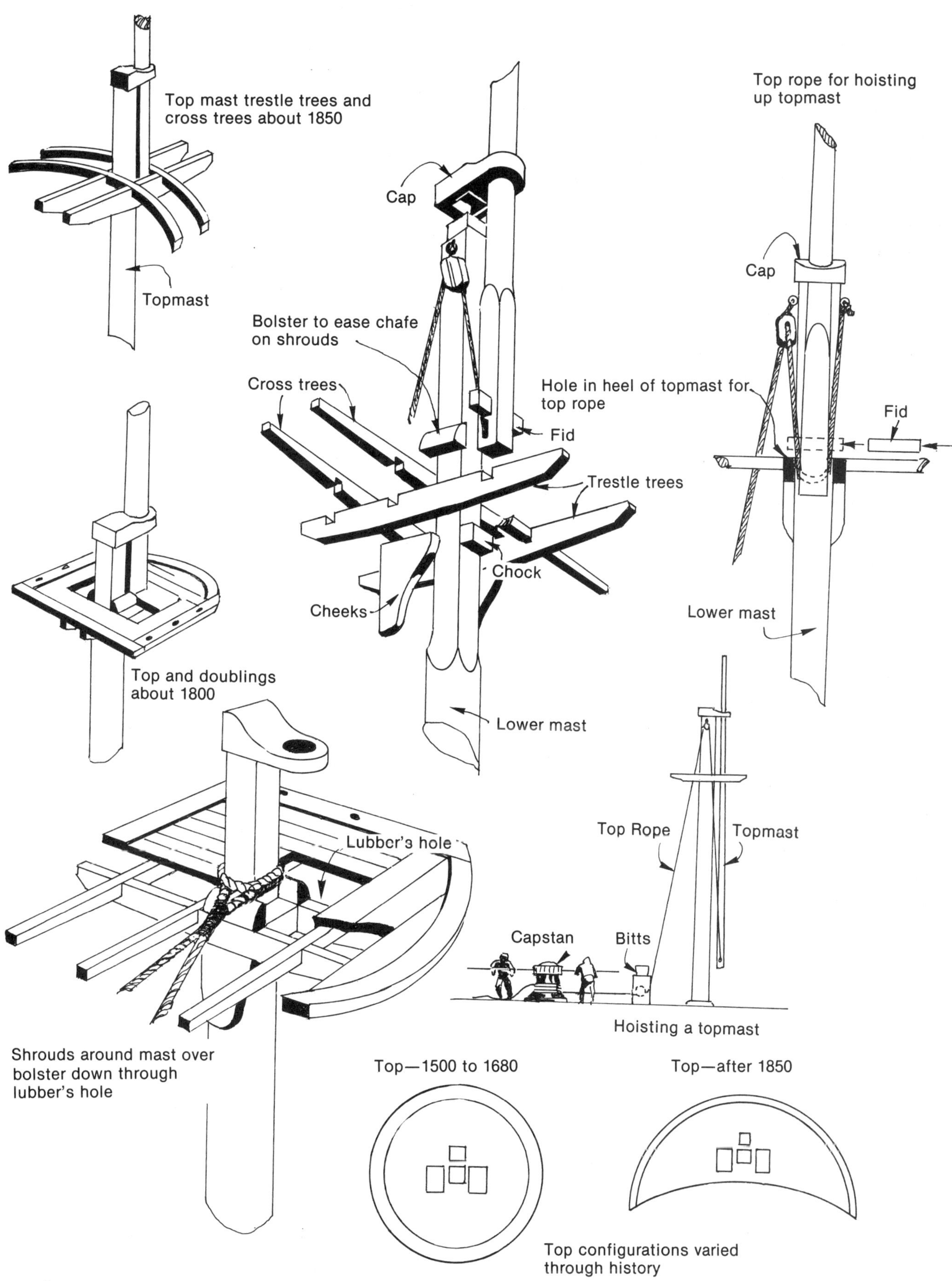

35

YARDS

The yards or yardarms of a ship were rigged like so many crosses of a 'T' up the masts of a square rigger. The sails were bent (fastened) onto the yards. The yards and the sails were fitted out with lines, tackles, sheaves, cleats and other gear for maneuvering the system about.

Early yard arms were rigged exclusively with hemp rope while later, chain and steel cable replaced rope where the strains were heaviest. Finally, iron replaced wood for the yard itself in some instances. Later yards may be distinguished from earlier ones by their jackstays—iron rods mounted with ring bolts on the top forward edge of the spar. The sail was tied to the jackstay in these later ships, while earlier the sail robands went around the whole spar.

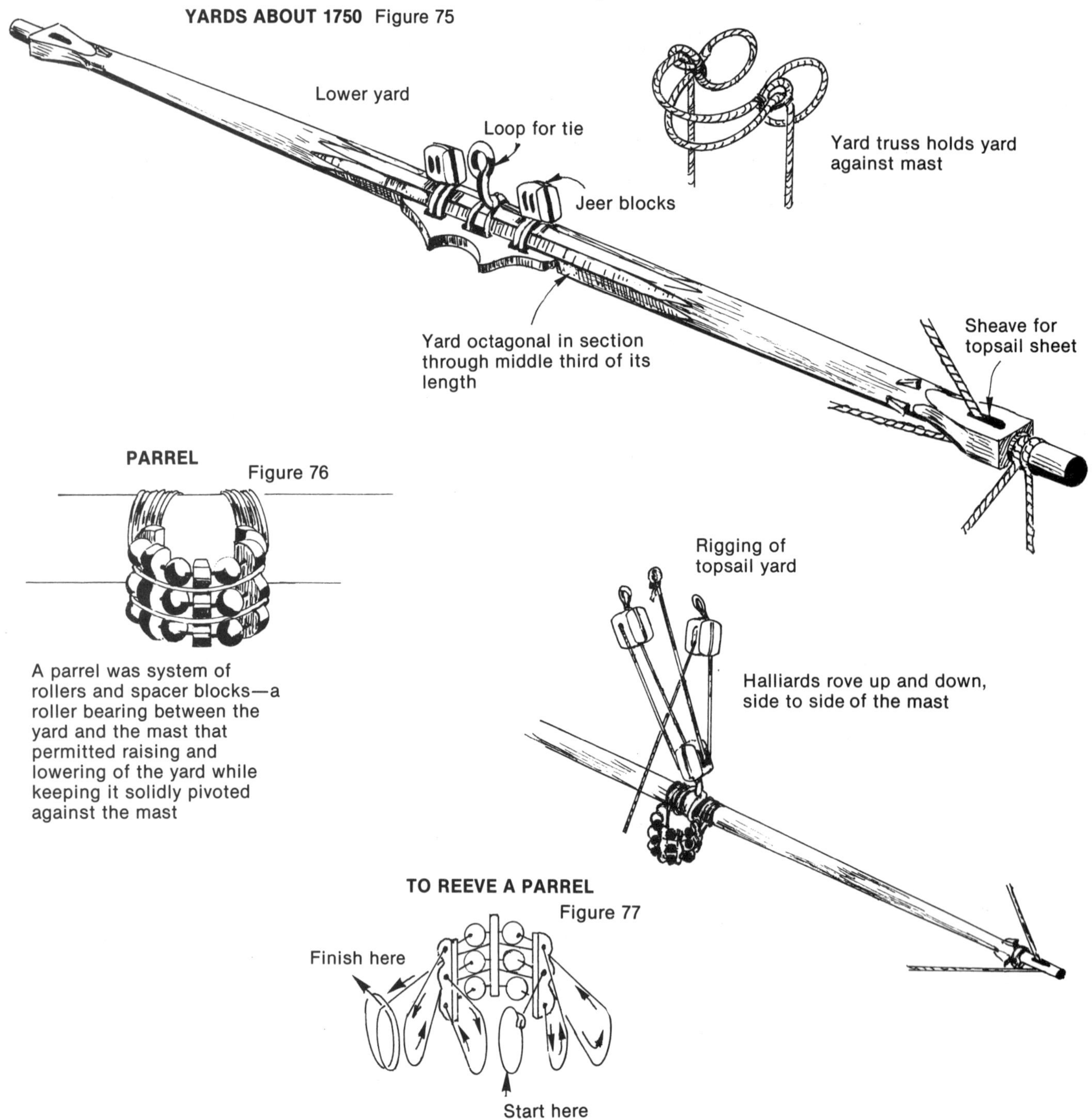

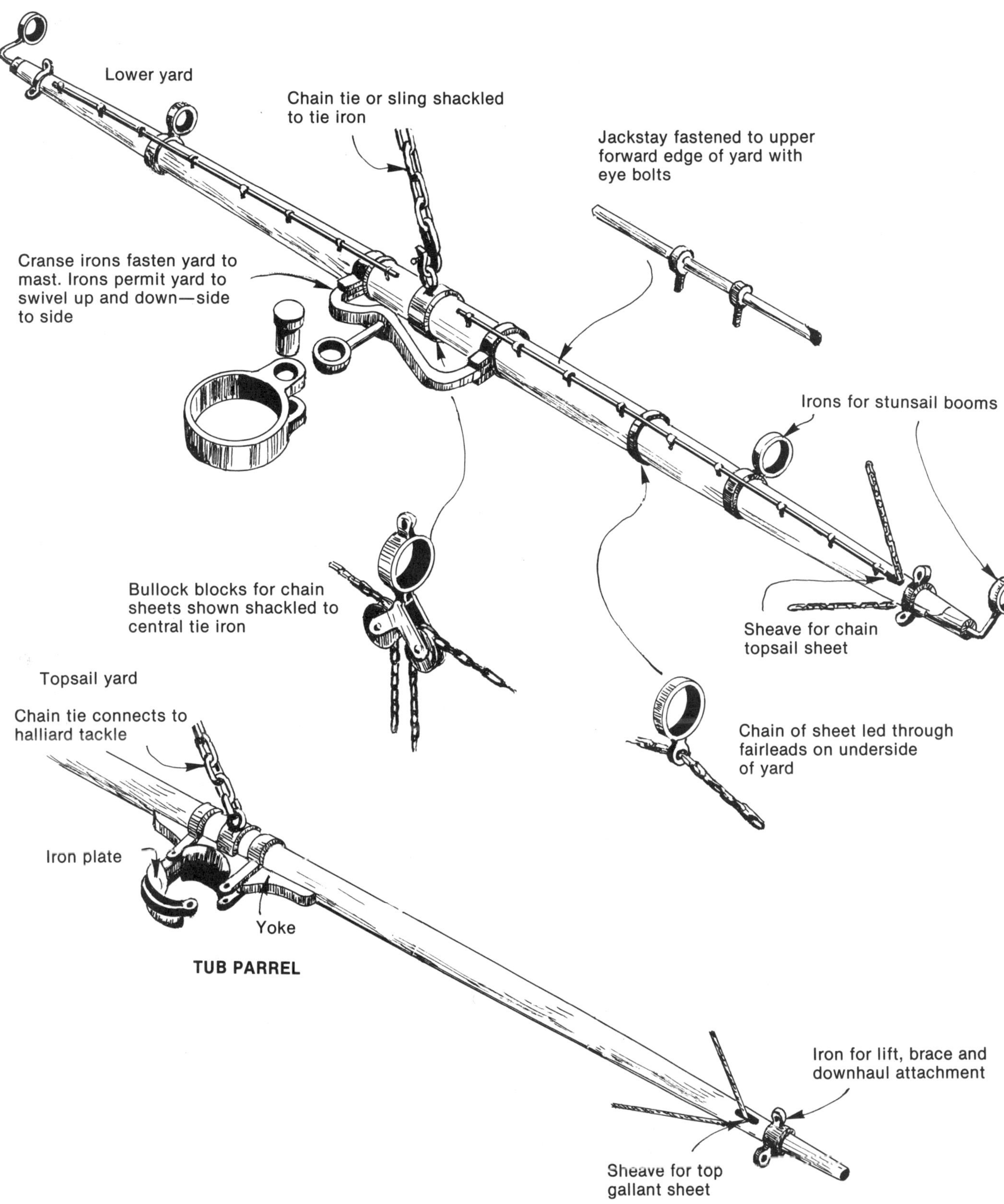
Lower yard
Chain tie or sling shackled to tie iron
Jackstay fastened to upper forward edge of yard with eye bolts
Cranse irons fasten yard to mast. Irons permit yard to swivel up and down—side to side
Irons for stunsail booms
Bullock blocks for chain sheets shown shackled to central tie iron
Sheave for chain topsail sheet
Topsail yard
Chain tie connects to halliard tackle
Chain of sheet led through fairleads on underside of yard
Iron plate
Yoke
TUB PARREL
Iron for lift, brace and downhaul attachment
Sheave for top gallant sheet

BOOMS AND GAFFS   Figure 78

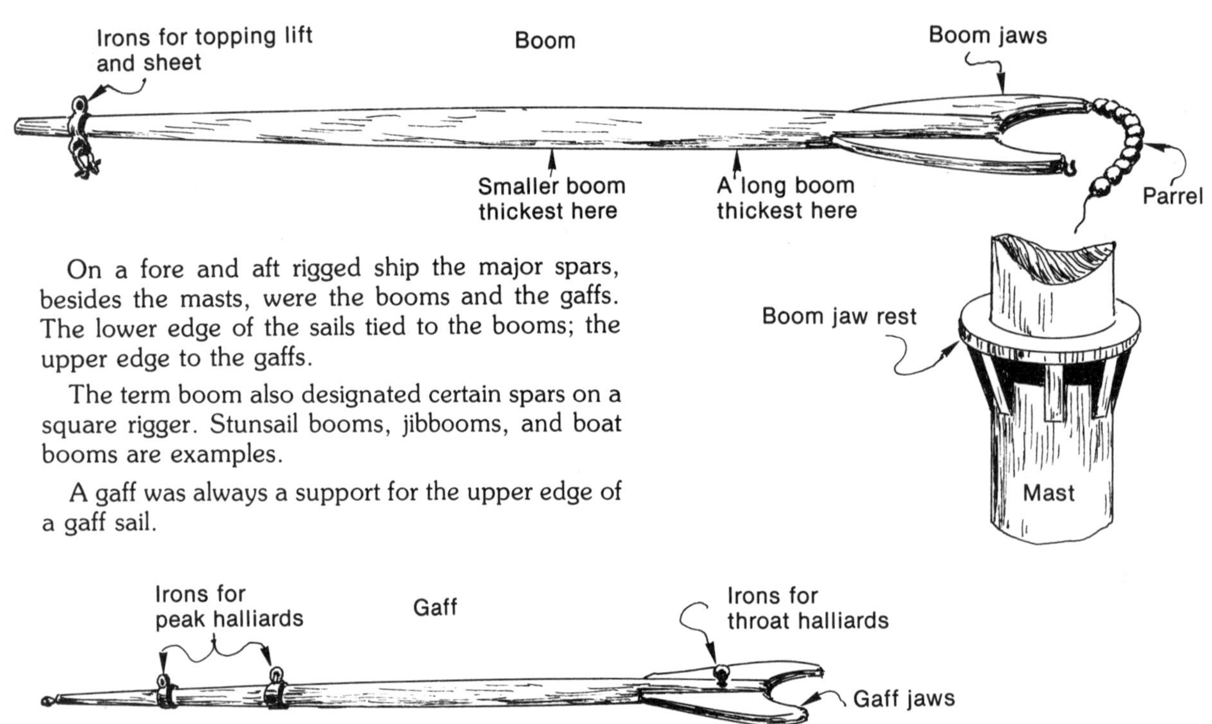

On a fore and aft rigged ship the major spars, besides the masts, were the booms and the gaffs. The lower edge of the sails tied to the booms; the upper edge to the gaffs.

The term boom also designated certain spars on a square rigger. Stunsail booms, jibbooms, and boat booms are examples.

A gaff was always a support for the upper edge of a gaff sail.

MAKING SPARS
Figure 79

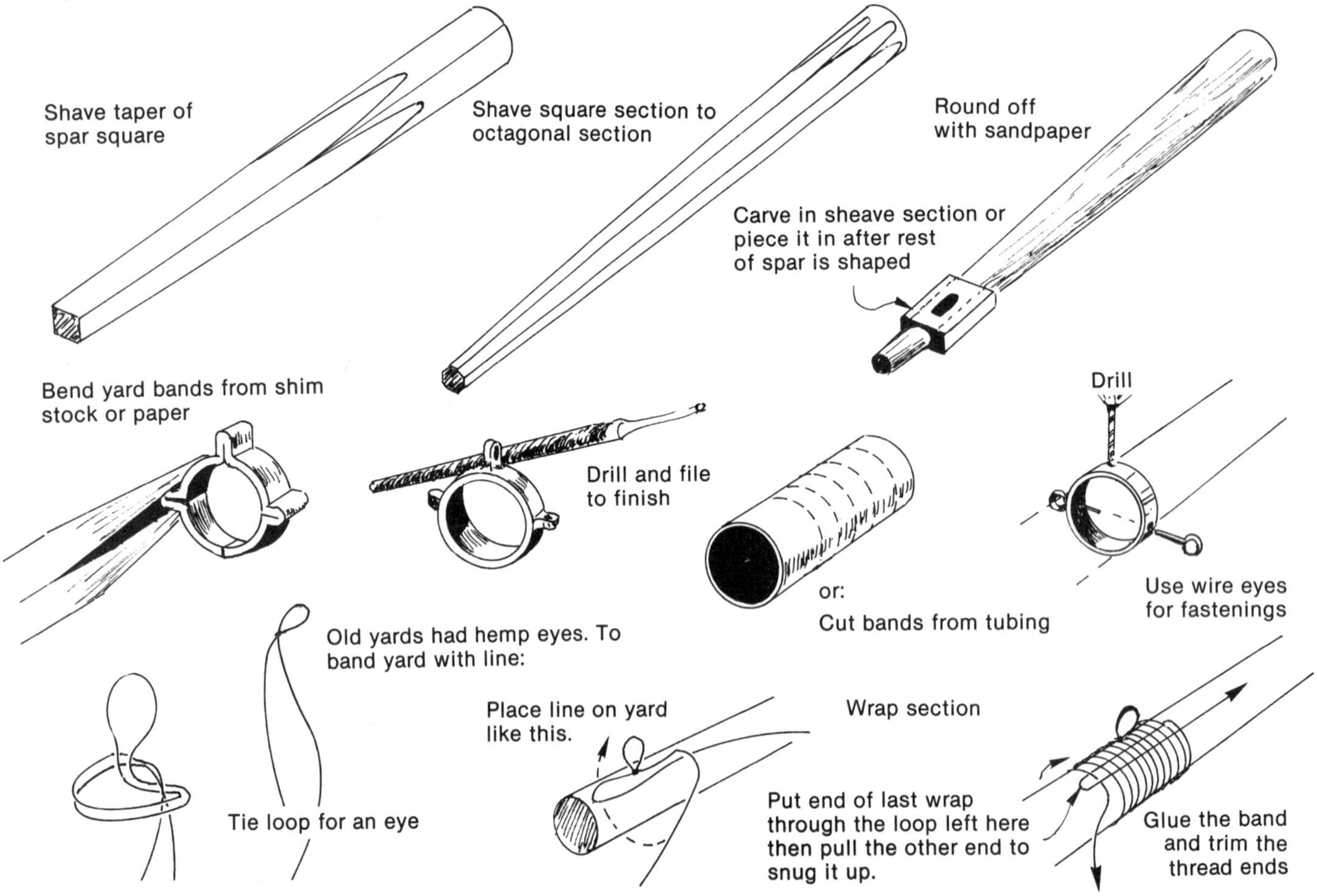

Yard bands and irons are available as adaptable prefabricated fittings.

THE BOWSPRIT AND OTHER HEAD SPARS

A ship's bowsprit and other head spars, perhaps more than any other feature, identify her place in history.

In Columbus' day the bowsprit was a single spar rising at a fairly steep angle out over the stem. A single square sail was set on it called the spritsail.

In the 1600's the steeve (the angle of steepness of the bowsprit) of the bowsprit was not much lower, but a little mast was added to its end called the sprit topmast. The sprit topmast carried another square sail called the sprit topsail.

In the 1700's the square spritsails and the sprit topmast gave way to lower steeved bowsprits and a jib boom or system of jib booms which extended out ahead of the ship on the same line as the sprit.

The square sprit sails were replaced with triangular fore and aft sails called jibs.

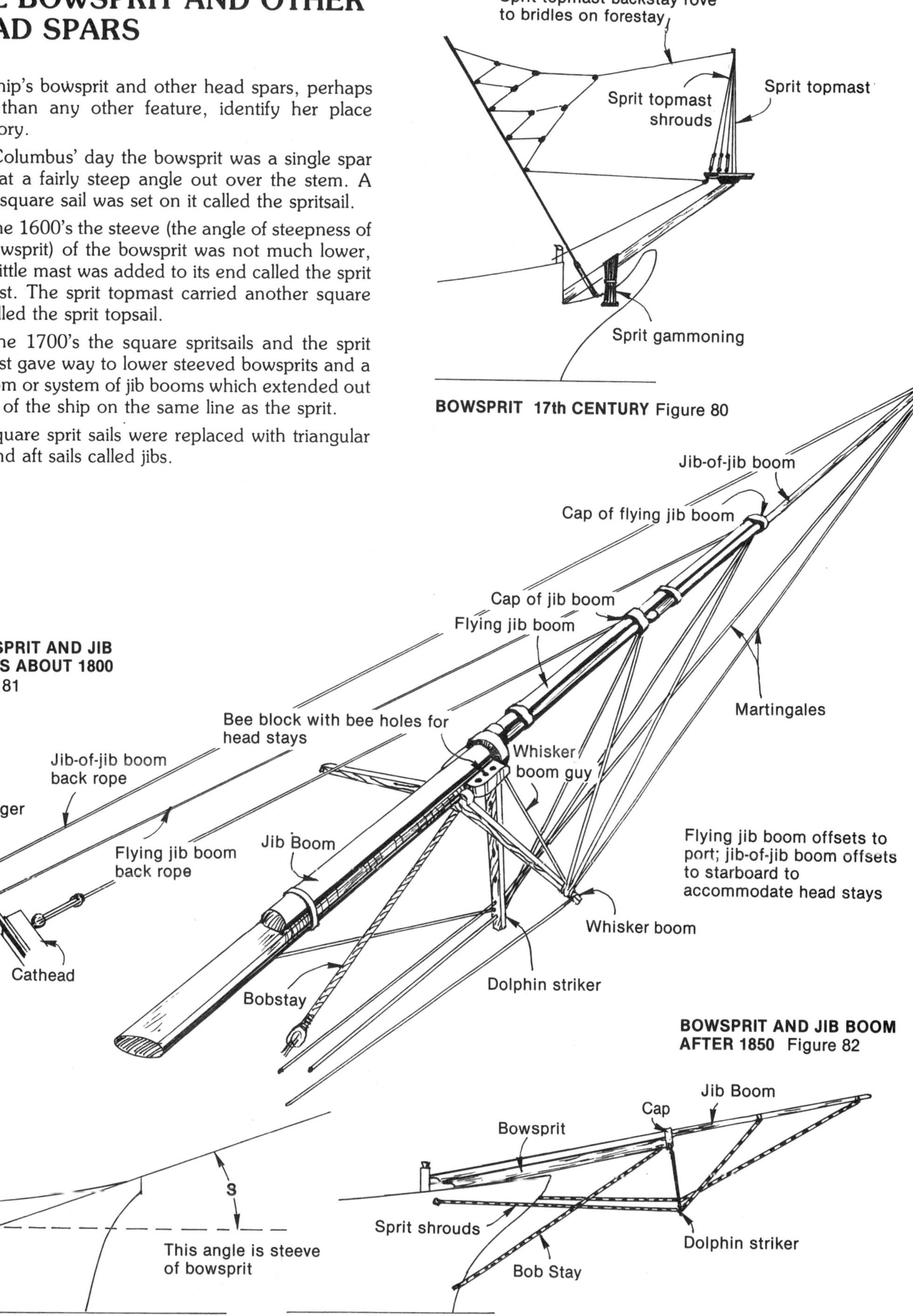

THE PRINCIPLES OF RIGGING

The common elements in the rigging of ships of all ages depend on the fact that masts must be held upright, spars must be attached so they can be maneuvered, and sails fitted out so they can be raised, lowered, set or furled and otherwise manipulated to catch the wind just right. In principle, the techniques and nomenclature for doing all these. things have not changed significantly in 500 years.

A ship's rigging breaks into two parts—the standing rigging and the running rigging.

STANDING RIGGING

Standing rigging was that which held up the masts and the bowsprit. This rigging was more or less permanently installed and was much heavier than the running rigging. Hemp standing rigging was preserved with a treatment of tar while many lengths of the lines were served,—wrapped round and round in snug turns with stout, tarred string called marlin.

By 1850 many elements of standing rigging were made from chain and wire cable.

Standing rigging consisted mainly of a system of shrouds and stays. The lower end of a stay was attached somewhere along the center line of the ship forward of the mast it supported. The upper end attached to the mast somewhere near the top.

Shrouds ran aft from the mast top down to the ship sides—to the channels or "chain wales"

The whole set up formed a stout three-sided pyramid with the mast in the middle (Figure 84).

The higher masts were supported the same way except that the shrouds led to the edge of the lower mast's top and futtock shrouds under the top took on the job of the chain plates. The stays of the higher masts led forward along the centerline of the ship, as did the lower stays, and tied off on a head spar or at points around the cap of a more forward, lower mast.

Upper masts often were fitted with backstays that came down to the ship side like shrouds but further aft.

Rigging lines, particularly those made of hemp, stretched and shrunk with changes in the weather. It was necessary therefore, to be able to adjust the tension on them. Tension on the shrouds was adjusted through a system of deadeyes and laniards. Deadeyes were oval blocks of hardwood with three holes drilled through them. A deadeye was fastened to the lower end of the shroud and another to the channel with an extension to the ship side called the chain plate. The two deadeyes were laced together with a laniard, a comparatively thin rope. Shroud tension was adjusted by slacking or tightening up the laniards. (Figure 85)

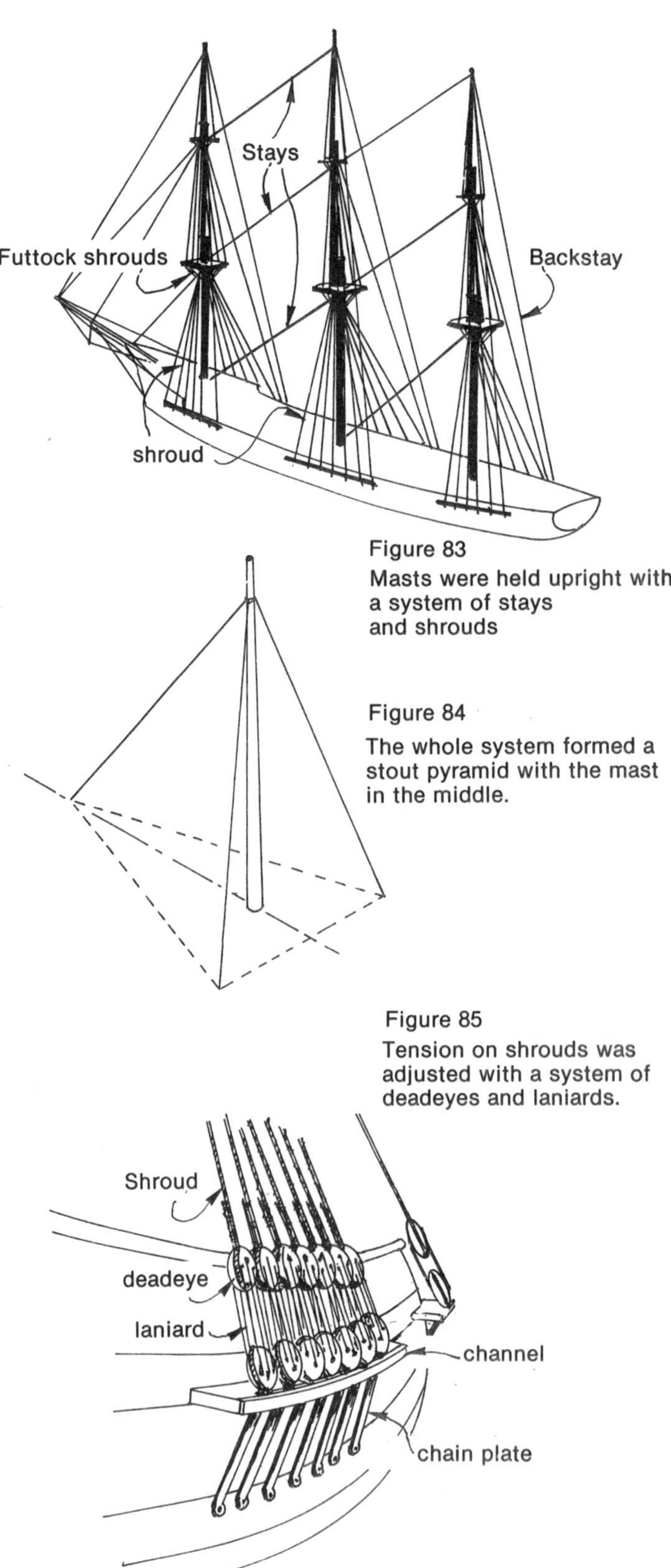

Figure 83
Masts were held upright with a system of stays and shrouds

Figure 84
The whole system formed a stout pyramid with the mast in the middle.

Figure 85
Tension on shrouds was adjusted with a system of deadeyes and laniards.

Round deadeye

Oval deadeye

Dead block

Heart

These fittings are available as prefabricated units.

Turnbuckle

MAKING DEADEYES Figure 87

1. Drill

2. Shape

3. Saw

4. Finish

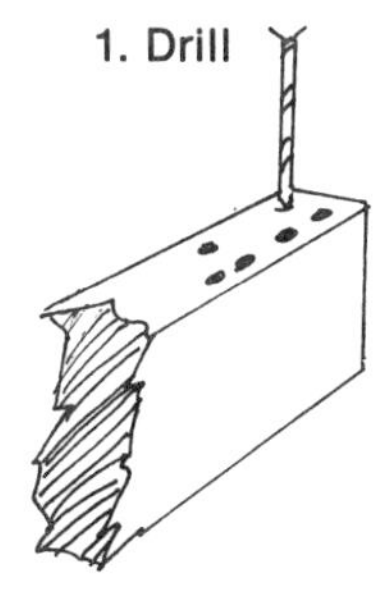
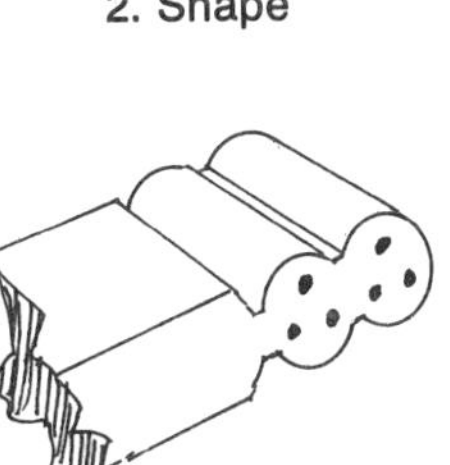
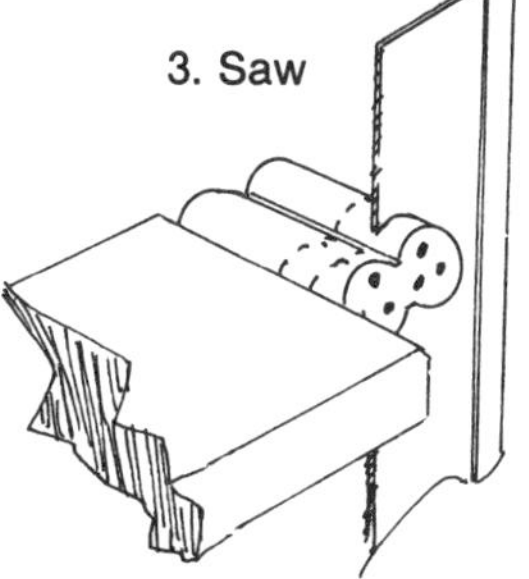
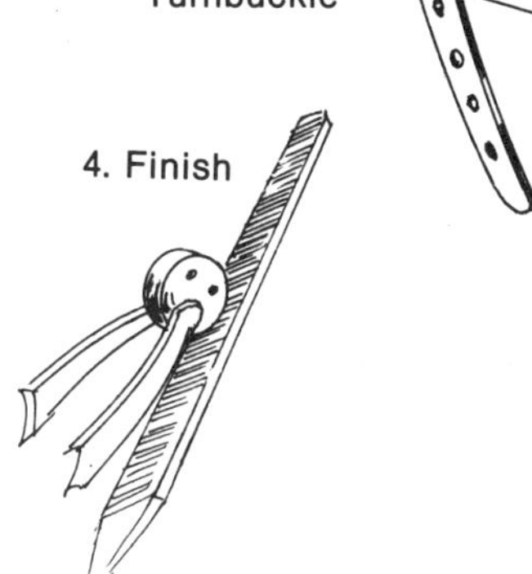

ROVING DEADEYES Figure 88

Outboard view

Inboard view

RATLINES Figure 89

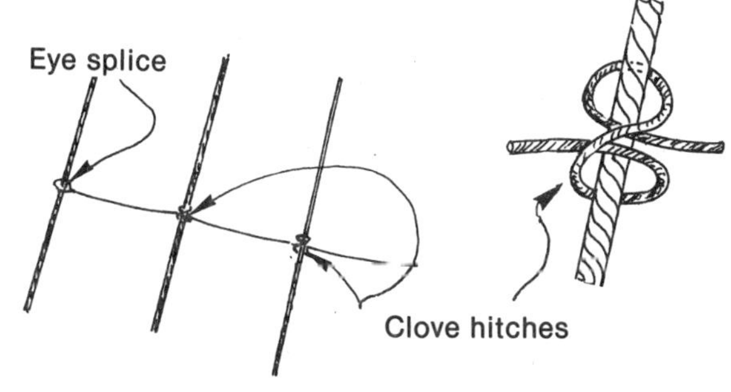

Stays were similarly adjusted, though instead of deadeyes, hearts were sometimes used. A heart was a more or less triangular shaped doughnut of hardwood. The laniards went through the holes of the doughnuts, the heavy lines around the outside edges.

The stays of a vessel were the heaviest lines in her rigging. The main and fore stays of a ship were cable laid lines sometimes 6 or more inches in diameter.

Most standing rigging was cable laid in contrast to "Z" or rope laid line. The difference between the two was the direction in which the strands were twisted. The strands of a cable were twisted clockwise; a rope counter-clockwise. (Figure 90)

Shrouds most always were rattled down. That is they were fitted up with ratlines—rope ladders by which sailors climbed into the upper rigging. (Figure 89). The ratlines of older ships were exclusively rope. Later wooden sheer poles made up the first rung of the ratlines above the deadeyes. Finally some ships were completely rattled down with wooden rungs.

After 1900 more efficient turn buckles began to replace deadeyes, hearts, and laniards as trimming devices for the shrouds and stays. Most modern yachts use turnbuckles for this purpose.

DETAILS OF STANDING RIGGING

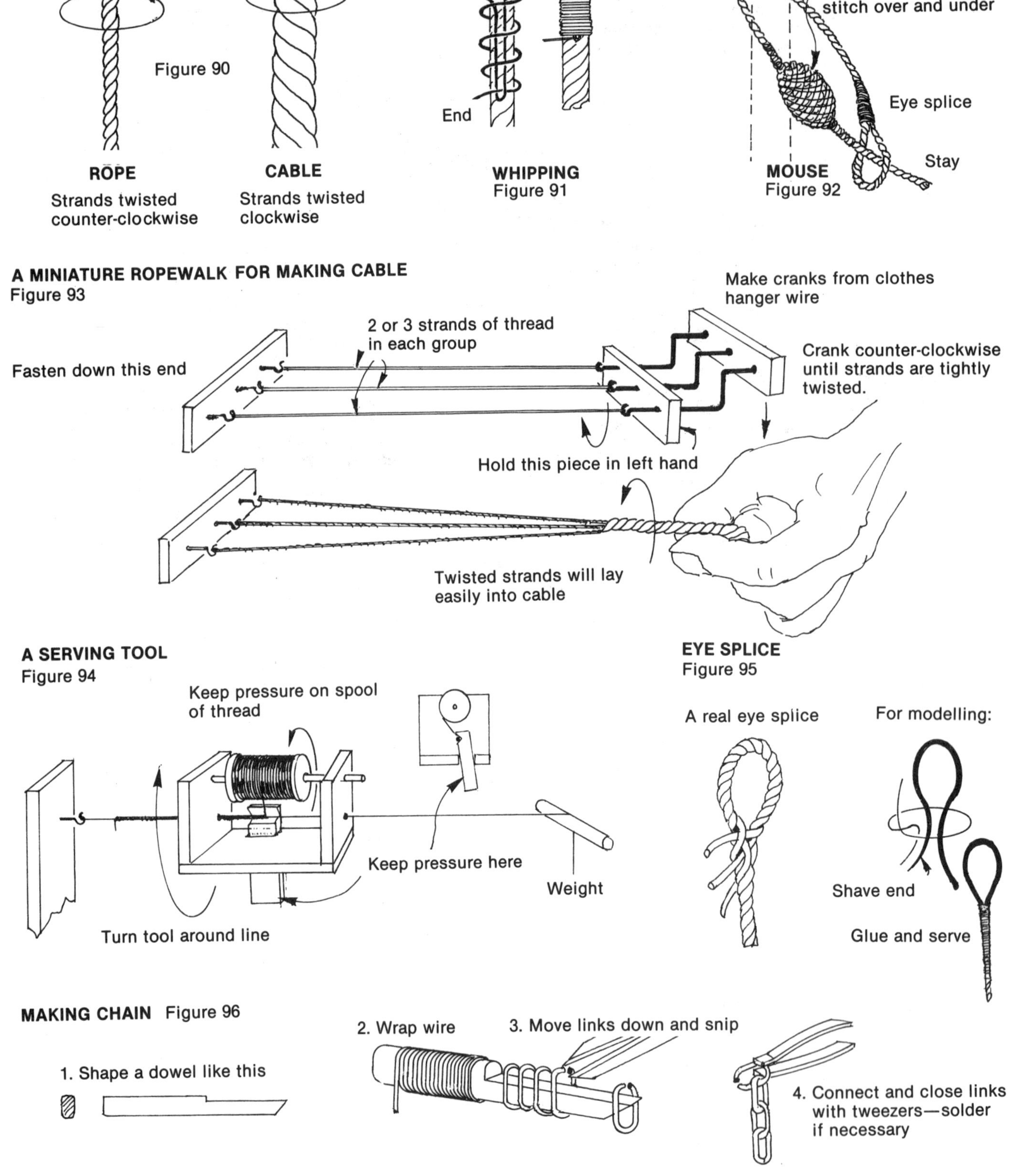

BOWSPRIT STANDING RIGGING Figure 97

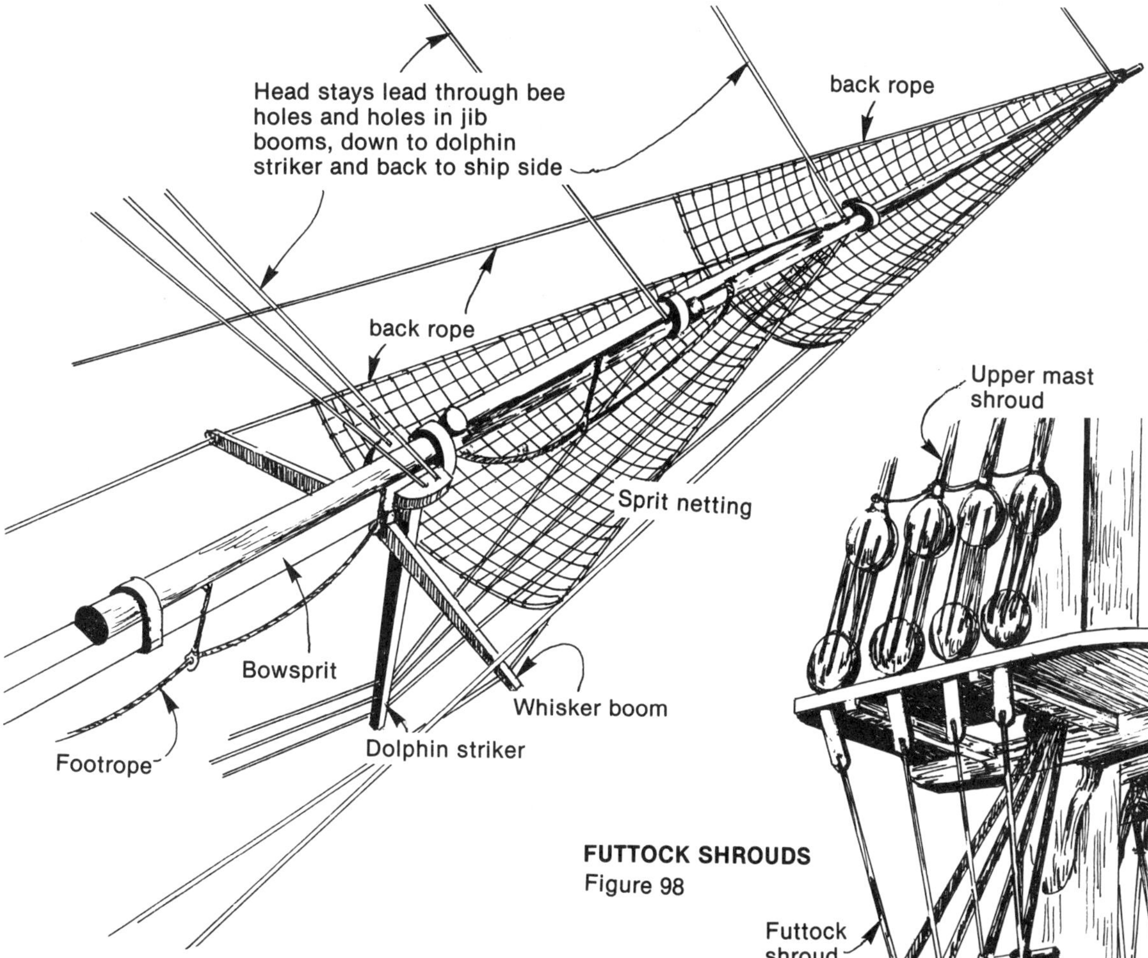

FUTTOCK SHROUDS
Figure 98

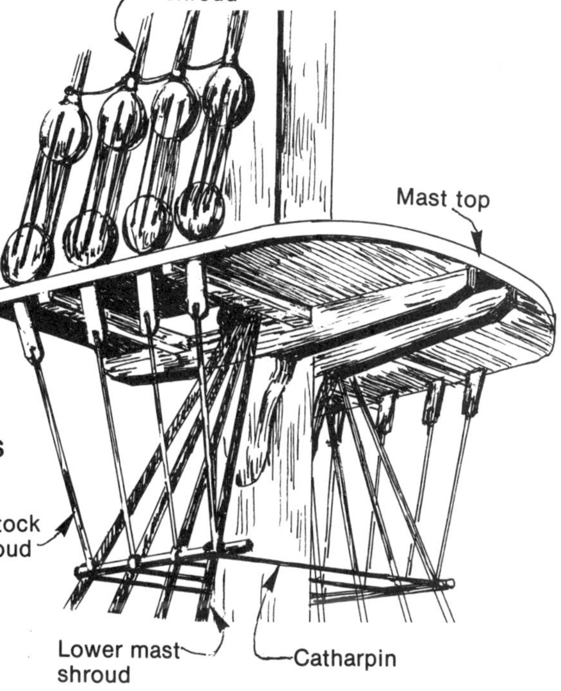

FOOTROPES Figure 99

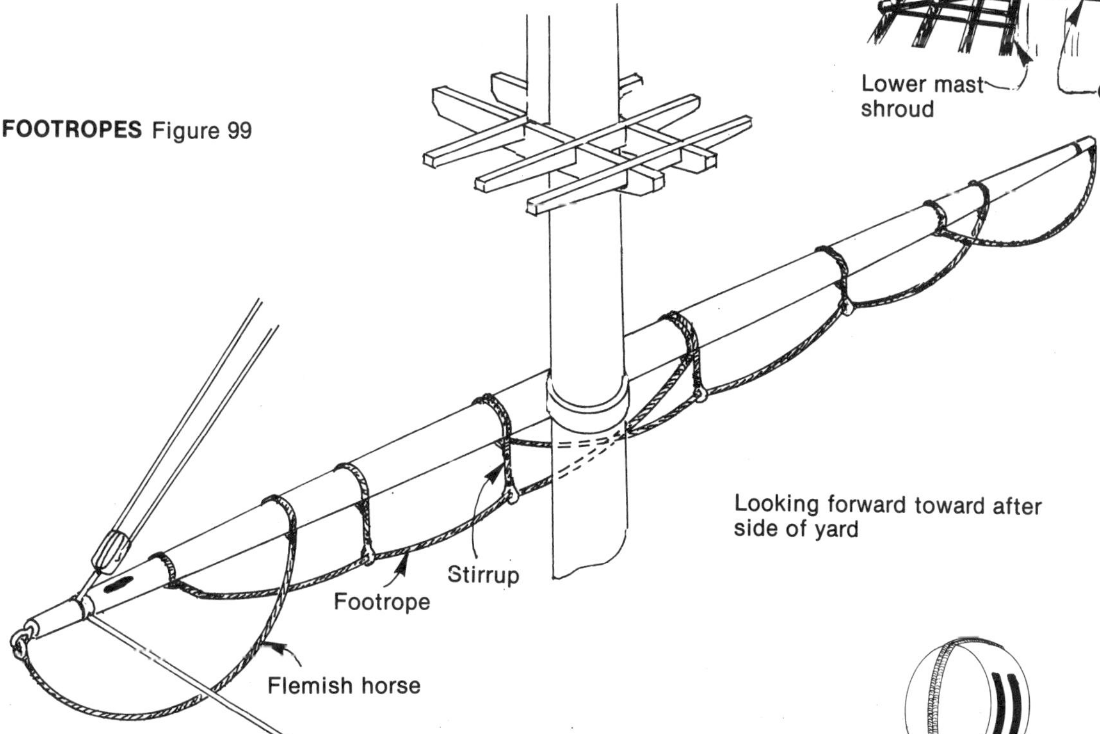

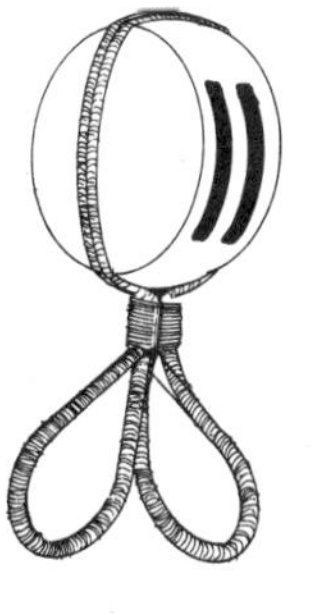

RUNNING RIGGING

The running rigging of a ship was the sum of the lines that did the hoisting, lowering, and trimming of the ship's operating gear.

The central elements of the running rigging were blocks and tackles. A block consisted of one or more sheaves, or grooved wheels mounted on an axle in a wood or metal shell. The block formed a roller bearing and guide for leading a rope around corners or back and forth through other blocks.

Blocks through the centuries took on a wide variety of shapes and sizes, some of which are illustrated here. Older blocks had wooden shells and external hemp strops. More modern blocks had metal or wood shells and internal metal strops.

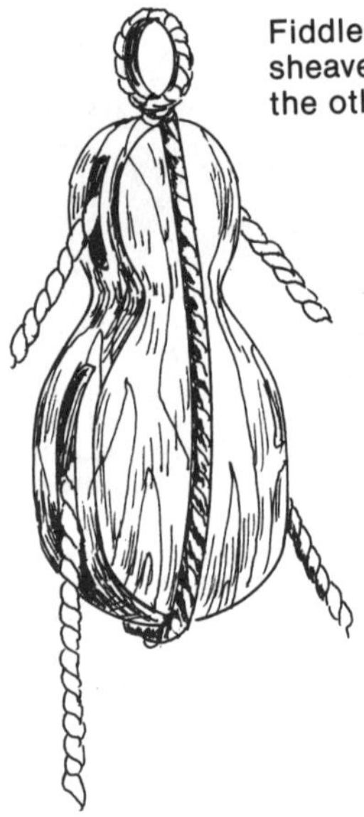

Blocks with an attachment loop on the bottom as well as the top are called becket blocks, the lower loop being referred to as the becket.

EXPLODED VIEW OF A BLOCK Figure 100

Fiddle block has two sheaves one over the other

17th century block

Sheet block with sister hooks

Figure 101

Gammon block

Snatch block

Figure 102

Double block Triple block Quadruple block

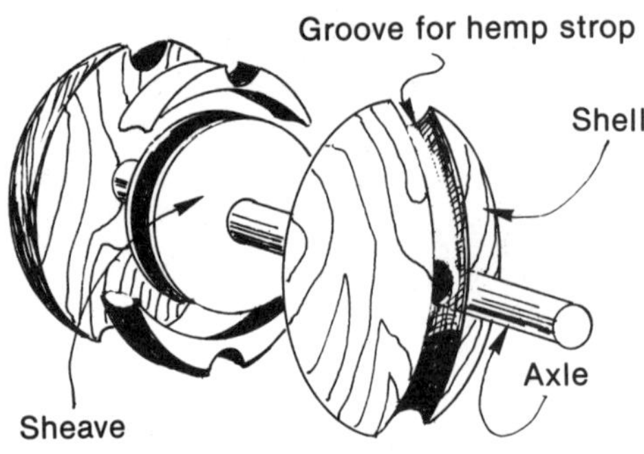

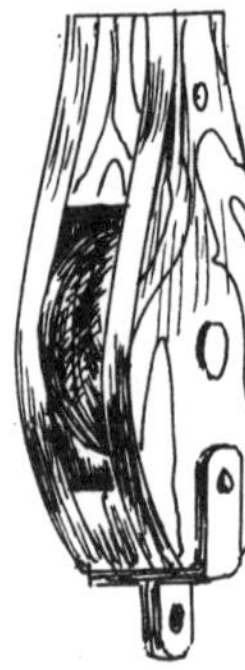

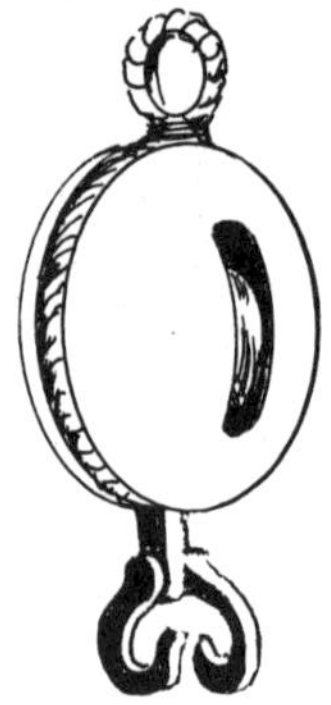

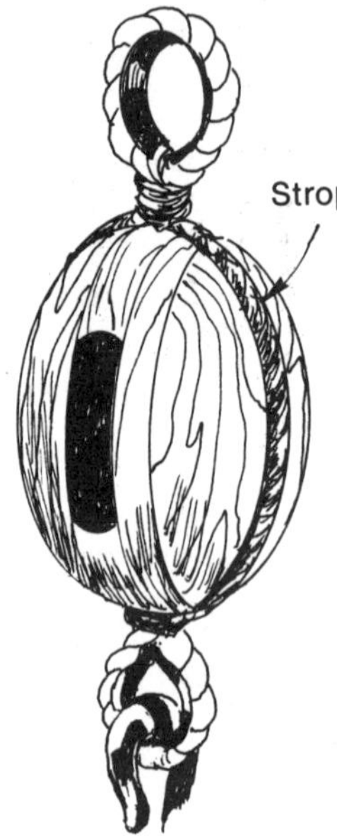

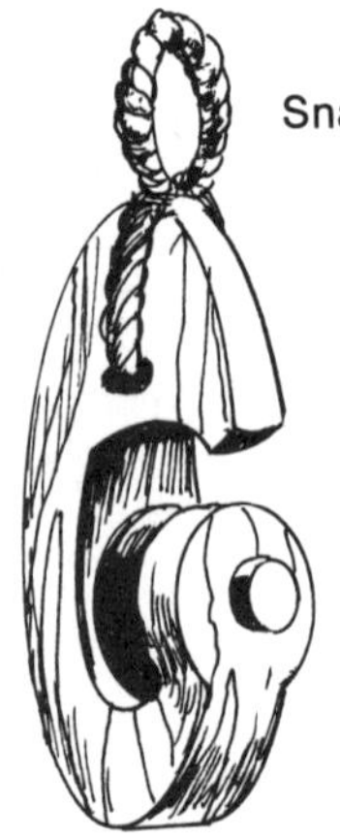

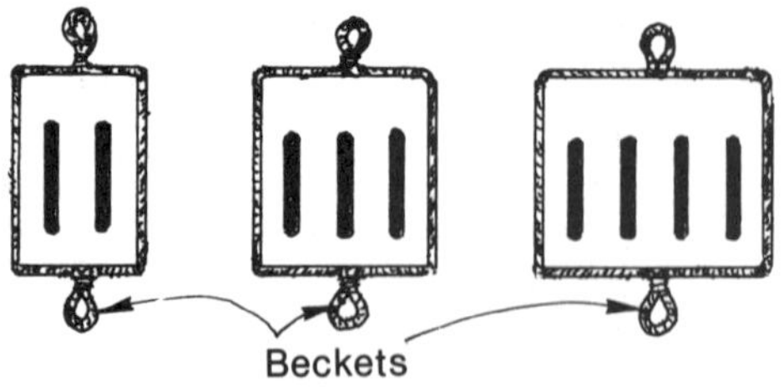

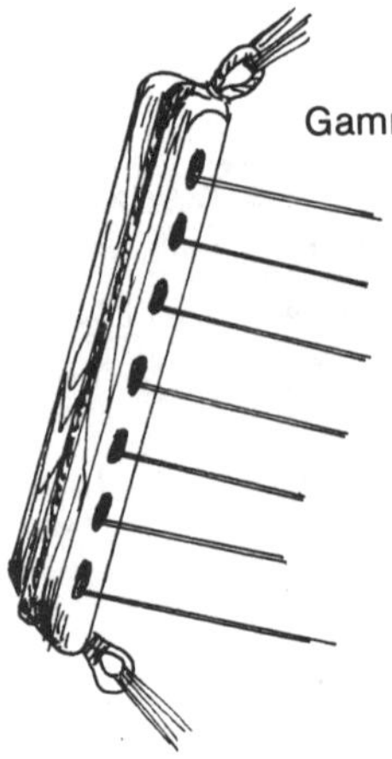

MAKING BLOCKS Figure 103

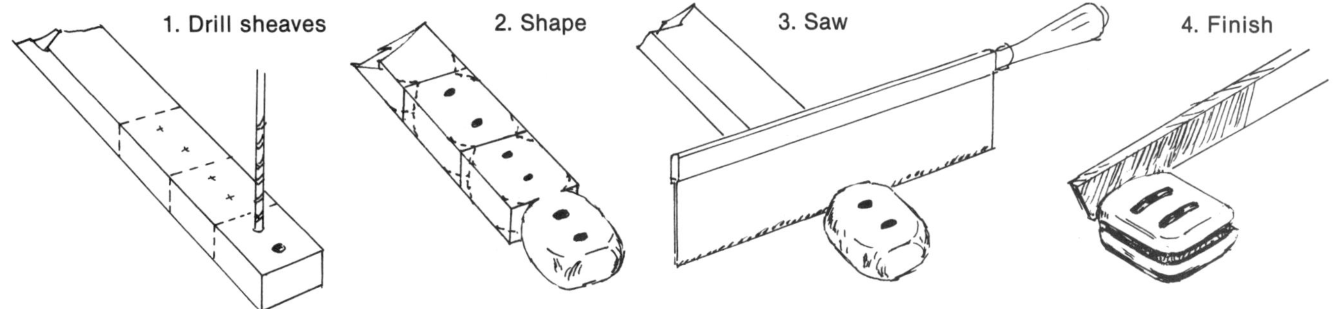

Blocks are available as prefabricated fittings.

STROPPING BLOCKS—HEMP Figure 104

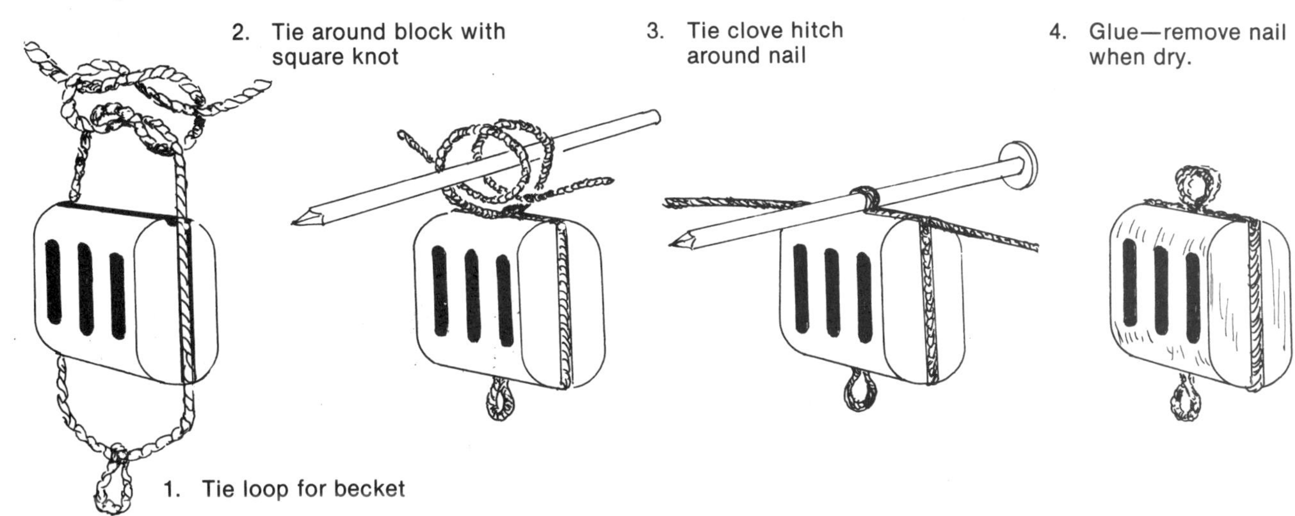

STROPPING BLOCKS—METAL Figure 105

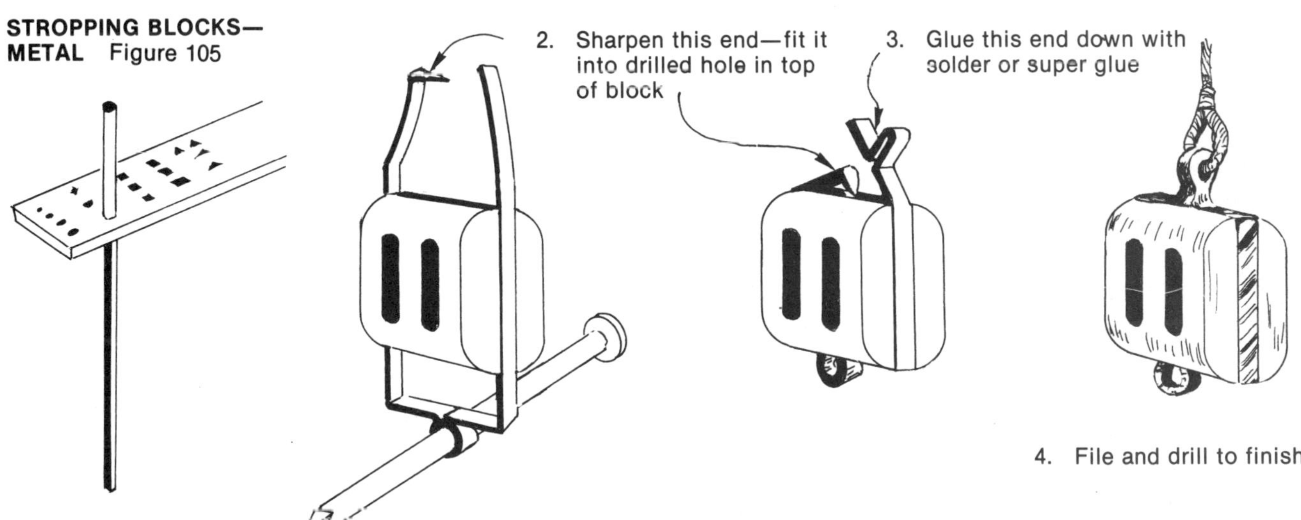

FITTINGS Figure 106

Rope, cable, wire and chain were fastened to the ship, to blocks, and to other lines in many different ways.

Among the fittings on the ship or its spars were eye bolts, ring bolts, pad eyes, cleats, kevils, and pin rails. Some of these fastenings we have discussed in the section on deck furniture.

Blocks were equipped with hooks, sister hooks, clip hooks and various kinds of swiveled rings.

Shackles attached lines or chains to various eyes.

Rope and cable was spliced into all sorts of configurations. An eye splice was a common method for fitting a loop to the end of a line. (Figure 95)

Finally, a sailor had a vocabulary of dozens of different knots.

Many of these details of rigging are of interest to the modeller only in so far as they add to his understanding of what is going on though excellent models seldom include more than simplified versions of these various attachments. Their size, in scale, is too small. The few knots shown in figure 108 should serve most if not all of a model's requirements, while carefully modelled blocks, fair leads, bee blocks, shackles and so forth add much to a model's effect if the scale is large enough to make them discernible.

Line belayed to pin

Pin rail with belaying pins

Bulls eye

Shackle

Wooden fair leads

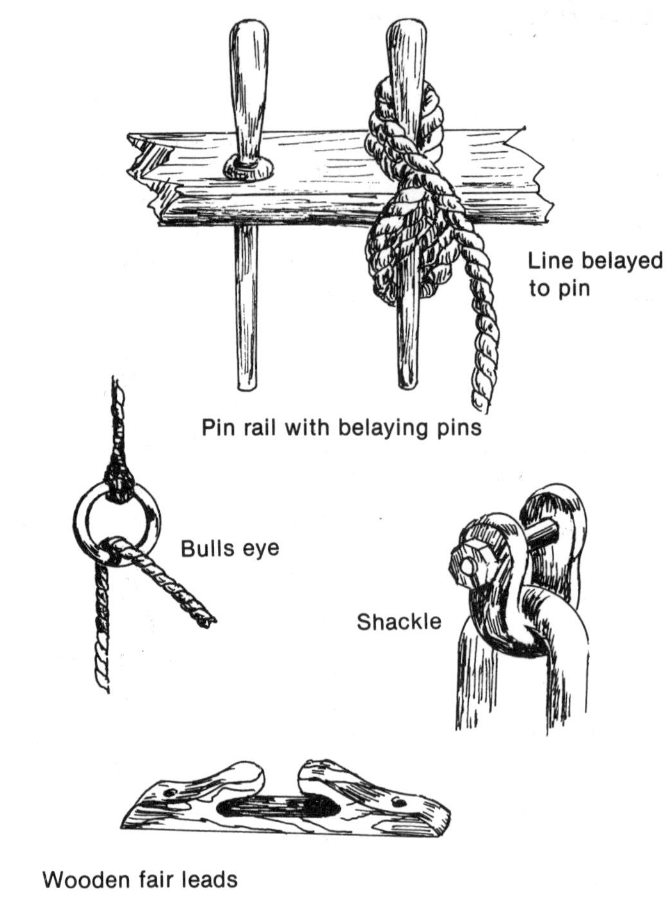

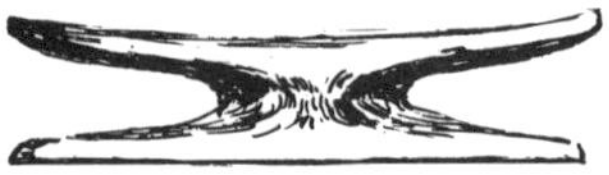

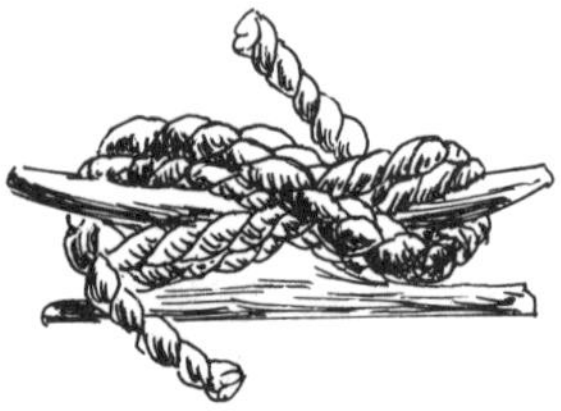

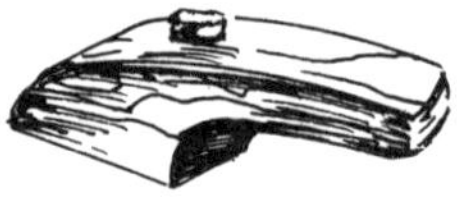

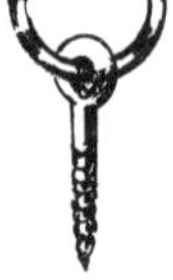

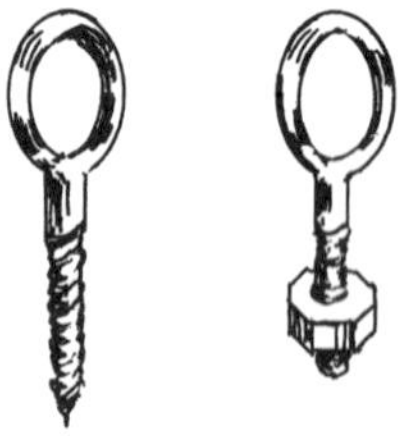

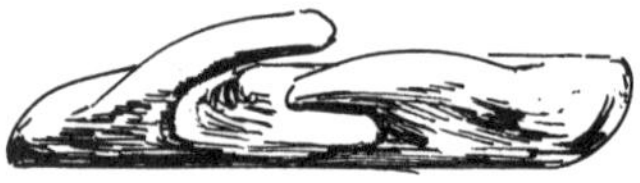

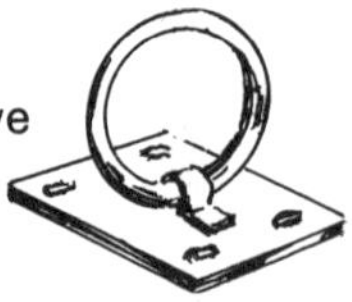

Ring bolt

Eye bolts

Cleat

Modern metal fair lead

Pad eye

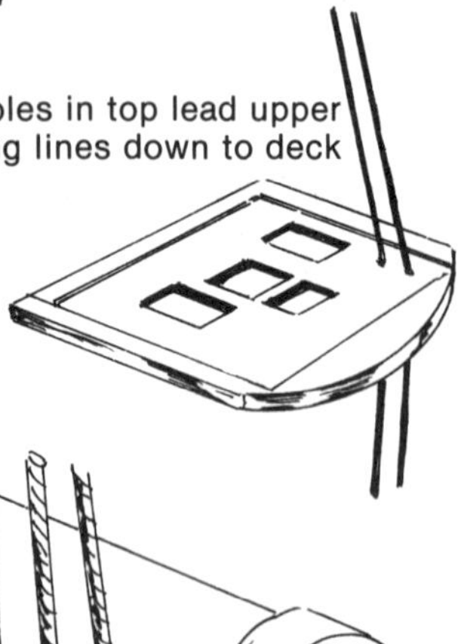

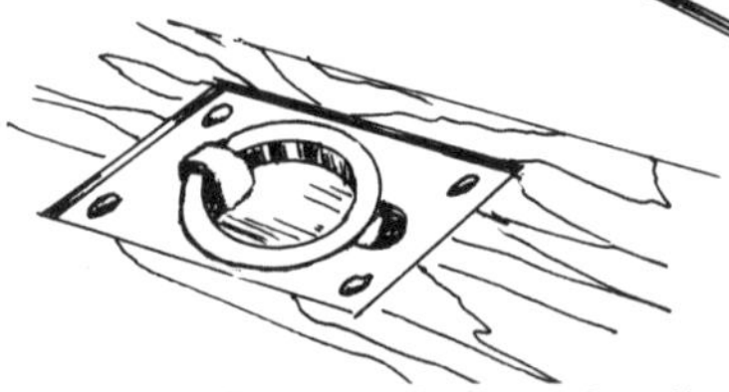

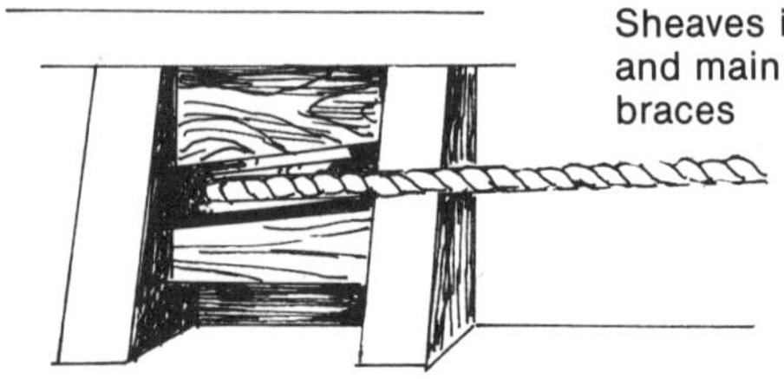

Pad eye designed to lie flush with deck

Bee holes in top lead upper rigging lines down to deck

Sheaves in bulwarks for fore and main course sheets and braces

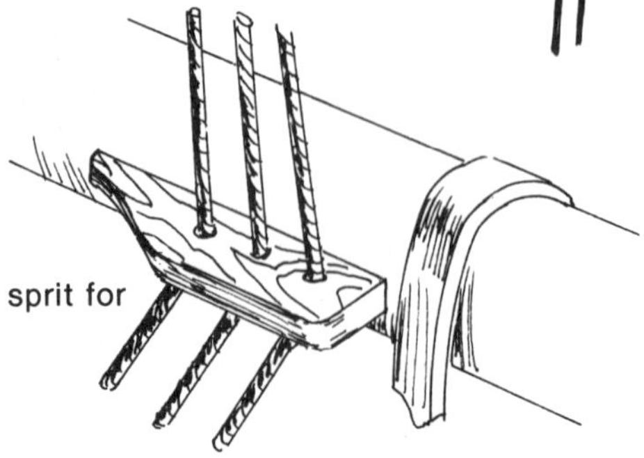

Bee block on bow sprit for head stays

A number of these fittings are available as prefabricated items.

TACKLES Figure 107

Tackles were systems of blocks and rope that increased the leverage or purchase of a line on its load. A multi-part tackle has the effect of dividing a heavy load into a series of lighter ones.

Figure 107 illustrates some of the tackle configurations common on many ships.

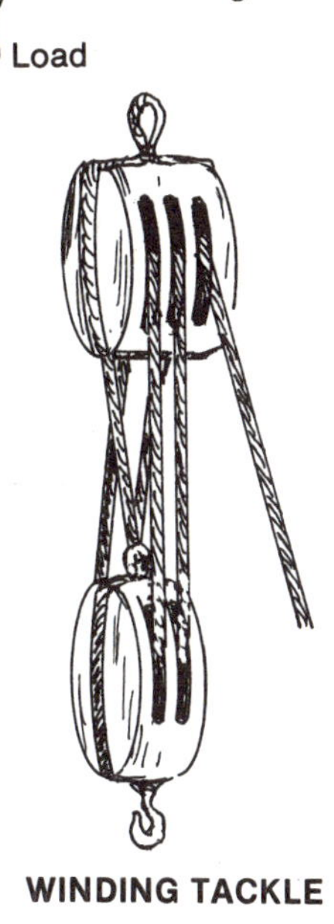

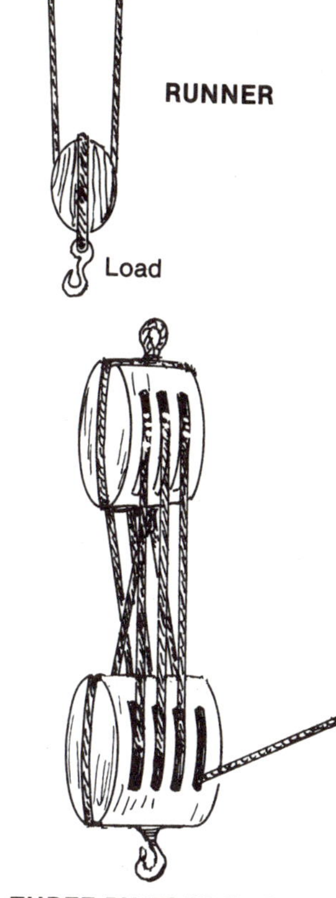

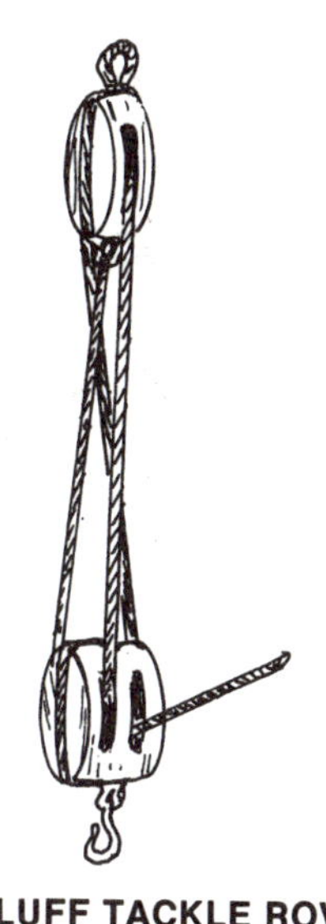

KNOTS Figure 108

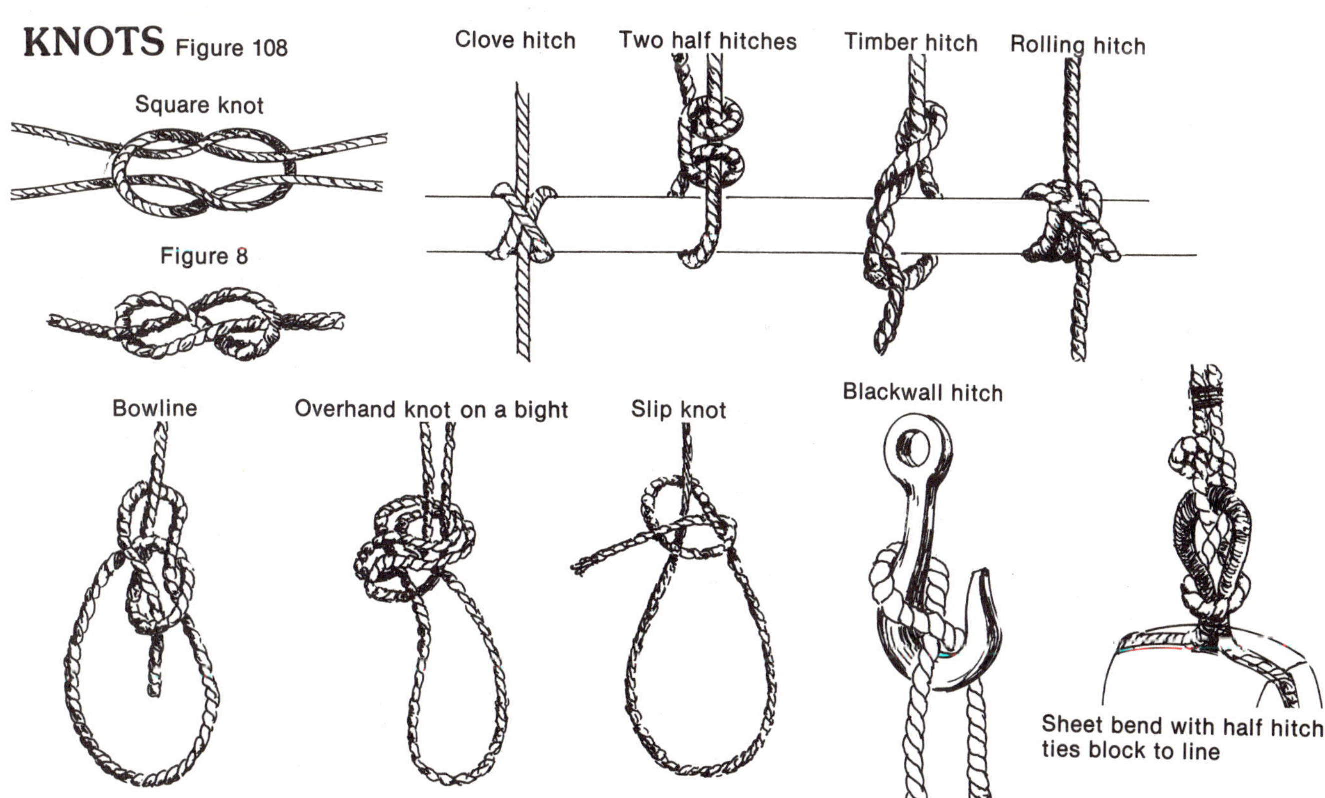

THE PRINCIPLE LINES

The ropes of a ship's running rigging are called lines not to be confused with the lines of the hull as described on page 8.

The lines fall into three functional classes:

1. Lines that hoist spars and other loads. This group includes top ropes, halliards, jeers, and mast and yard tackles. Ties, slings and trusses may also be classed in this group though they support the spars rather than hoist them up

2. Lines that maneuver yards and sails while the ship is under weigh. The braces hauled the yards fore and aft; the lifts tilted them up and down. The clew line hauled the lower outboard corner of a square sail up to the yard. The sheet pulled the same corner down and aft. The tack pulled the corner forward. The tack was fitted only to the lower sails.

A bowline hauled the windward edge of the sail forward.

3. Lines that furled (rolled up and stored) sails. Buntlines hauled up the lower edge (the foot) of a square sail. Leech lines hauled up the outer edges (the leeches). This group might also include the reefing gear which was used to reduce a sail's working area in strong winds. Reefing tackle, attached to a cringle part way down the sail's leech hauled the cringle up to the end of the yard. The sail then was tied all along the yard on a line starting at that point with short reefing ropes run through the sail on the reef band.

Finally, some yards and sails were equipped with downhauls, inhauls, and outhauls. Their names declare their function. (Figure 110)

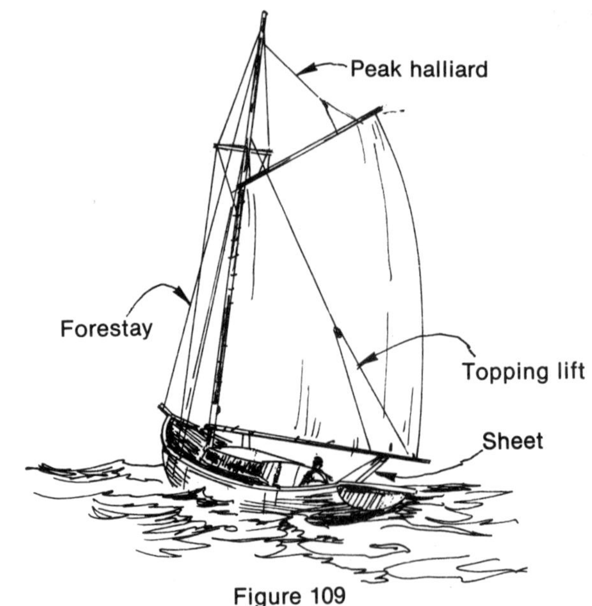

Figure 109

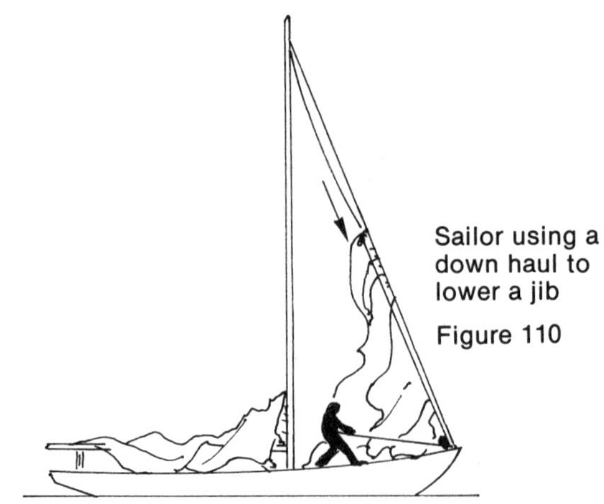

Figure 110

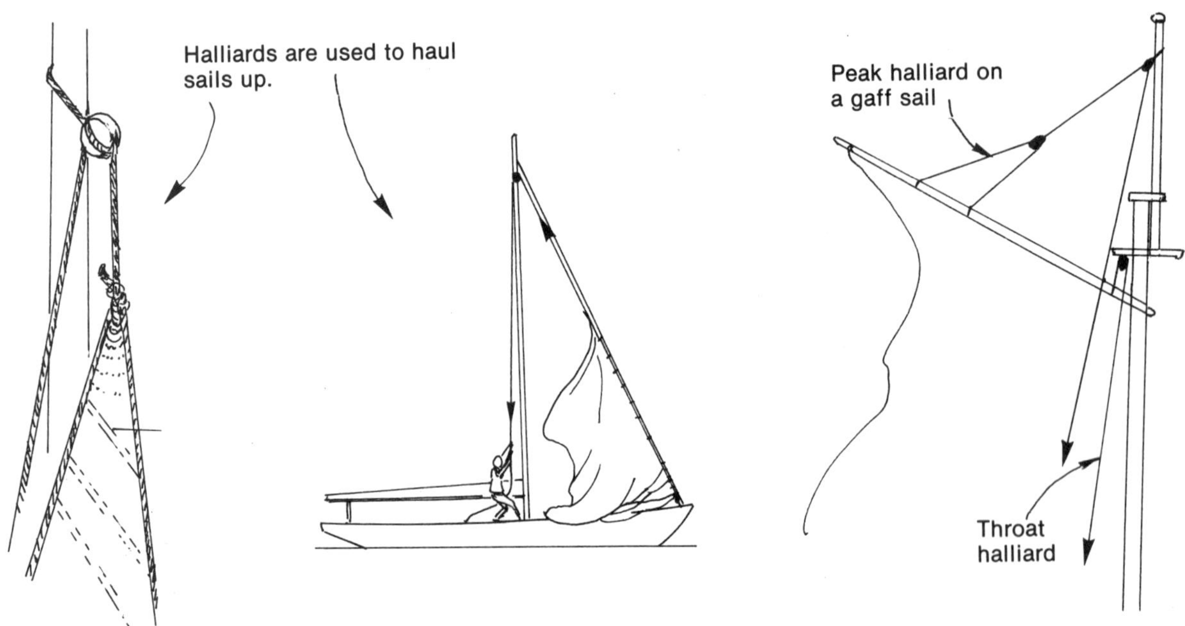

Figure 111

FORE AND AFT RIGGING

Some of the sails on a square rigger were set parallel with the line of the keel. These sails are called fore and aft sails. Among these are the jibs (head sails), stay sails, and the spanker.

A large class of ships including most modern yachts have all of their sails rigged fore and aft. Fore and aft running rigging is generally simpler than that of the square rigger, but the principle classes of lines are the same. Halliards hoist up the sails; downhauls and inhauls bring them down. Sheets handle the after lower corners of the sail though sometimes that corner is attached to a boom and the sheet attaches to the boom rather than the sail proper.

A few lines belong exclusively to the fore and aft rig. For instance, a topping lift raises the end of a fore and aft boom while a vang controls the outer end of a gaff.

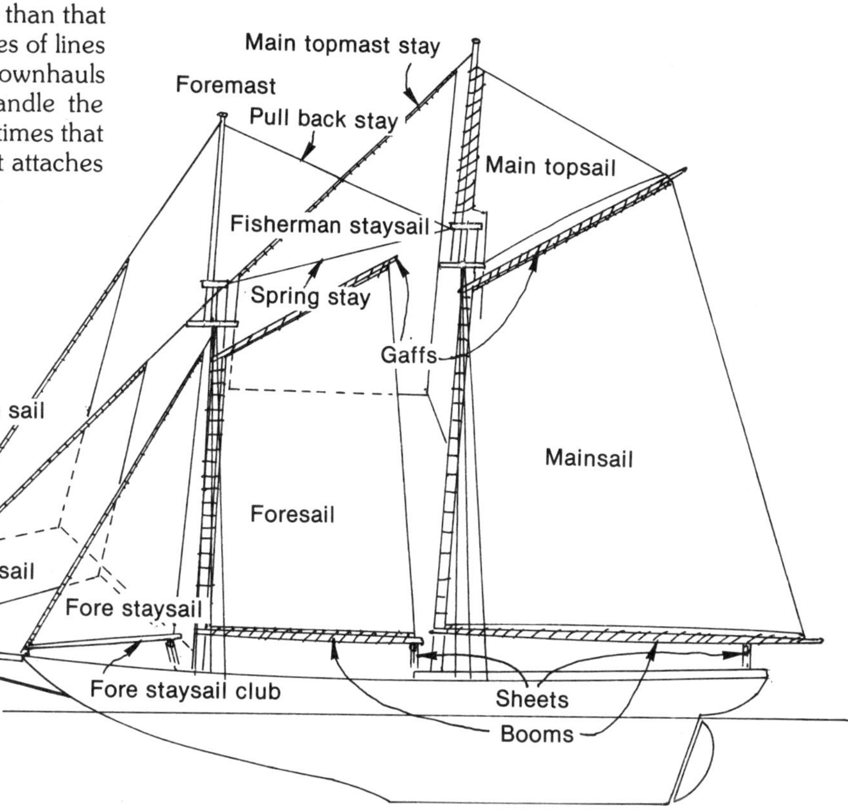

FORE AND AFT RIGGED SCHOONER
Figure 112

LINE THICKNESS

A ship's lines varied in thickness in proportion to the loads they were expected to carry.

An idea of where the heaviest loads of ship's running rigging lay may be gleaned from the following comparison of line sizes from a ship of about 1700.

For the sake of simplicity we have given a single, large dimension for certain lines which in fact would be composites of several line thicknesses rigged as tackles, pendants and the like.

2 inch line
Main jeers, Main top ropes, Main tack

1-1/2 inch line
Main topsail halliards, Main topmast top rope, Mizzen top rope, Mainsheet, Main brace, Maintop brace, Fore tack

1-1/4 inch line
Fore top halliards, Fore topmast top rope, Fore sheet, Fore top sheet, Mizzen tack

1 inch line
Mizzen top halliards, Mizzen topmast top rope, Main lift, Forebrace, Main top clew, Main course bowline, Main top bowline

3/4 inch line
Fore lift, Mizzen lift, Fore top brace, Main top brace, Mizzen (crojack) brace, Main top gallant sheet, Mizzen sheet, Mizzen top sheet, Main course clew, Fore bowline, Fore leech, Fore top leech, Main course, Leech, Main top leech, Mizzen course leech, Mizzen top leech

5/8 inch line
Main top gallant halliard, Mizzen top lift, Mizzen top brace, Fore topgallant sheet, Fore top clew, Mizzen clew, Mizzen top clew

1/2 inch line
Fore top lift, Main top lift, Fore clew, Fore top bowline, Mizzen bowline, Mizzen top bowline, Fore course bunt, Fore top bunt, Main course bunt, Main top bunt, Mizzen bunt, Mizzen top bunt

3/8 inch line
Fore topgallant lift, Main topgallant lift, Fore topgallant brace, Main topgallant brace, Fore topgallant clew, Main topgallant clew, Fore topgallant bowline, Main topgallant bowline, Fore topgallant bunt, Main topgallant bunt

TIES, JEERS, HALLIARDS Figure 113

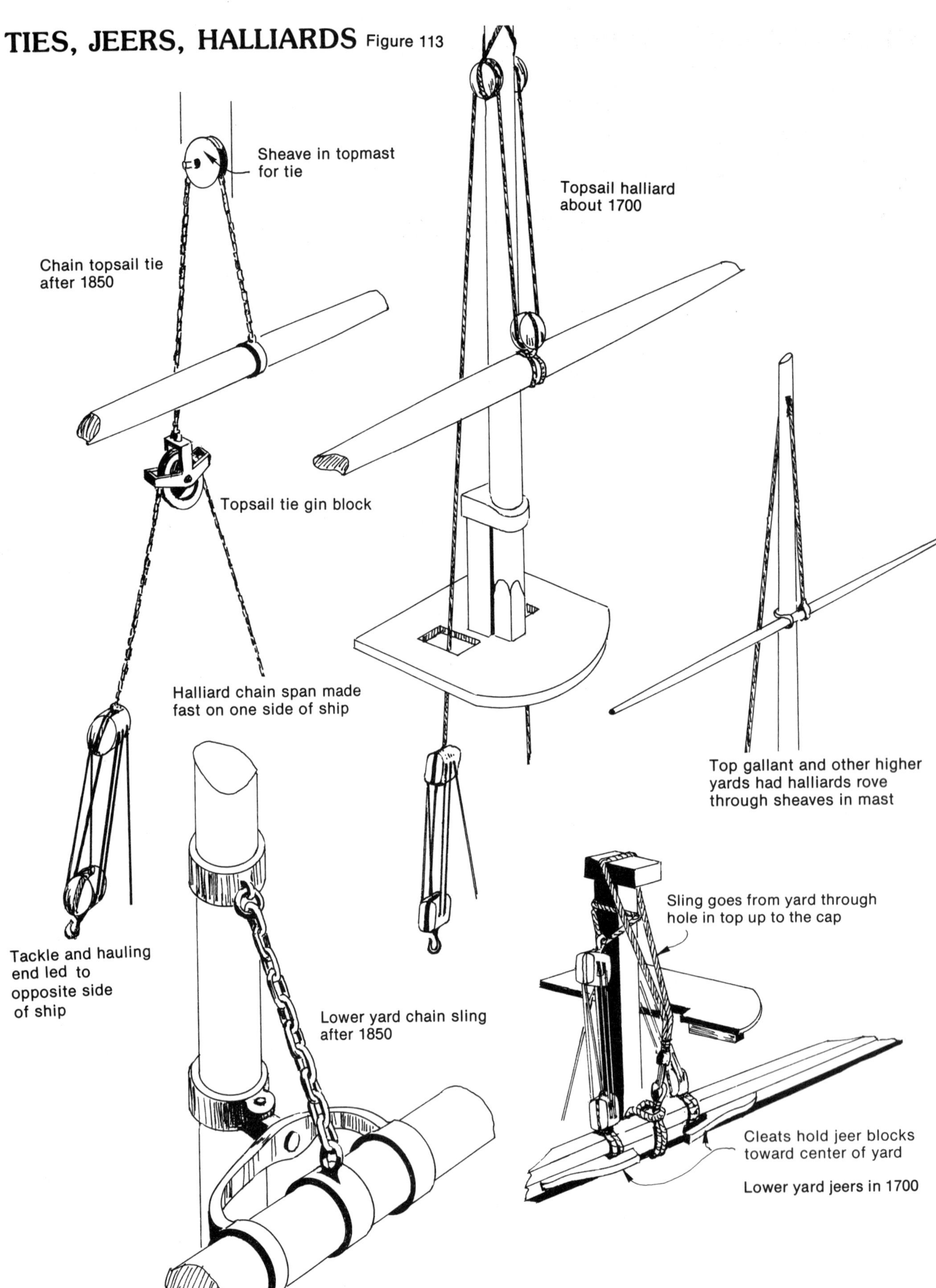
Sheave in topmast for tie
Chain topsail tie after 1850
Topsail halliard about 1700
Topsail tie gin block
Halliard chain span made fast on one side of ship
Tackle and hauling end led to opposite side of ship
Lower yard chain sling after 1850
Top gallant and other higher yards had halliards rove through sheaves in mast
Sling goes from yard through hole in top up to the cap
Cleats hold jeer blocks toward center of yard
Lower yard jeers in 1700

LINES FOR SAIL HANDLING Figure 114

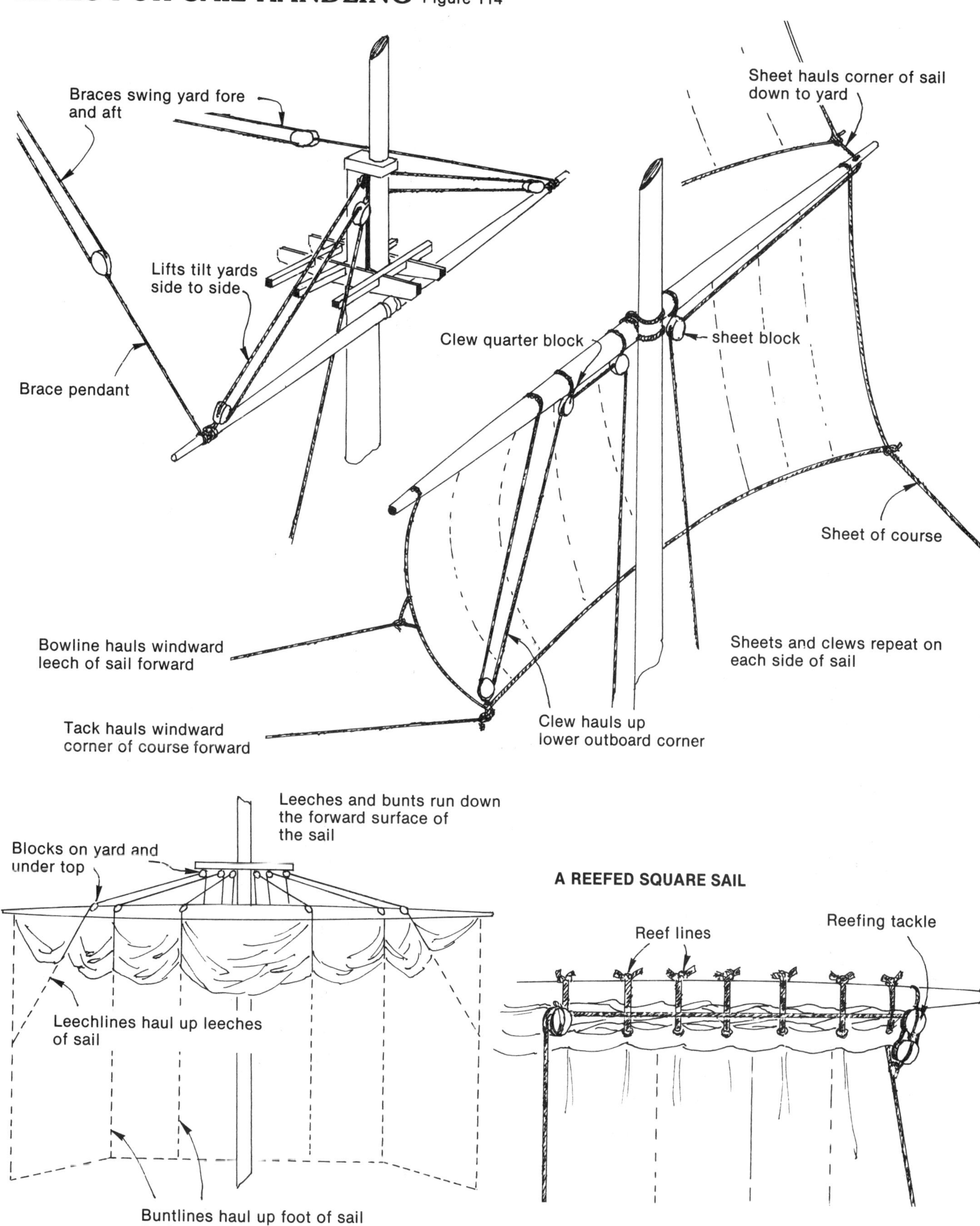

RIGGING THE MODEL

A real ship was rigged from fore to aft starting with the bowsprit, and modellers generally agree that this is the best way to rig a model as well.

The sequence outlined below may be used as a general guide.

The most important consideration in rigging a model is to be sure that irons, blocks and other fittings are in place on the yards, masts and hull before roving the lines. Trying to fit blocks under the tops, or pad eyes to the deck through a web of rigging is a headache at best; impossible at worst.

A little advance planning will save hours of aggravation.

STANDING RIGGING

Figure 115

Do not preassemble masts—rig them up one at a time like the real ship

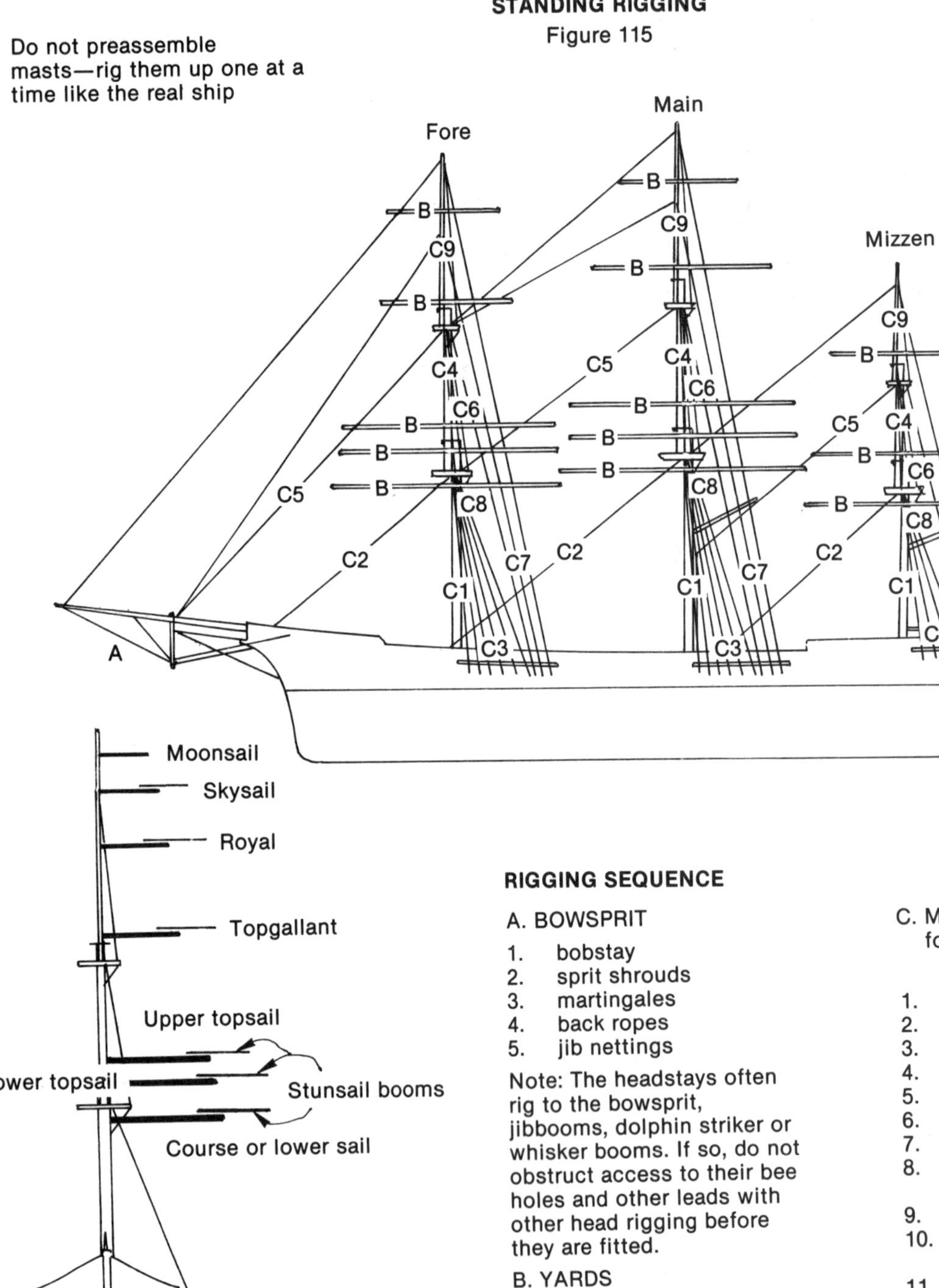

RIGGING SEQUENCE

A. BOWSPRIT

1. bobstay
2. sprit shrouds
3. martingales
4. back ropes
5. jib nettings

Note: The headstays often rig to the bowsprit, jibbooms, dolphin striker or whisker booms. If so, do not obstruct access to their bee holes and other leads with other head rigging before they are fitted.

B. YARDS

1. footropes
2. flemish horses
3. parrels
4. fit to mast

C. MASTS—start with foremast, work aft

1. set up lower mast
2. stay(s)
3. shrouds
4. set up top mast
5. stay
6. shrouds
7. backstays
8. futtock shrouds, catharpins
9. set up top gallant masts
10. Repeat procedures as with lower masts
11. ratlines
12. add crow's feet, gill guys, blocks and other fittings which attach to shrouds and stays.

RUNNING RIGGING

Will the model have sails or not? This decision must be made before going on with the running rigging.

Some modellers prefer to leave sails off on the grounds that they tend to obscure much of the model's other details, and otherwise "don't look right."

On the other hand, a model fitted with sails includes a lot of the interesting running gear that otherwise must be left off.

If a ship was scheduled to lie in port for some time her sails were unbent (taken off) and most of the running rigging was taken down with them. The model without sails is considered to be a ship in this "laid up" condition.

The running rigging sequence below includes all the lines for a model with sails. The lines marked with a star are those that would normally be left off if the sails are left off.

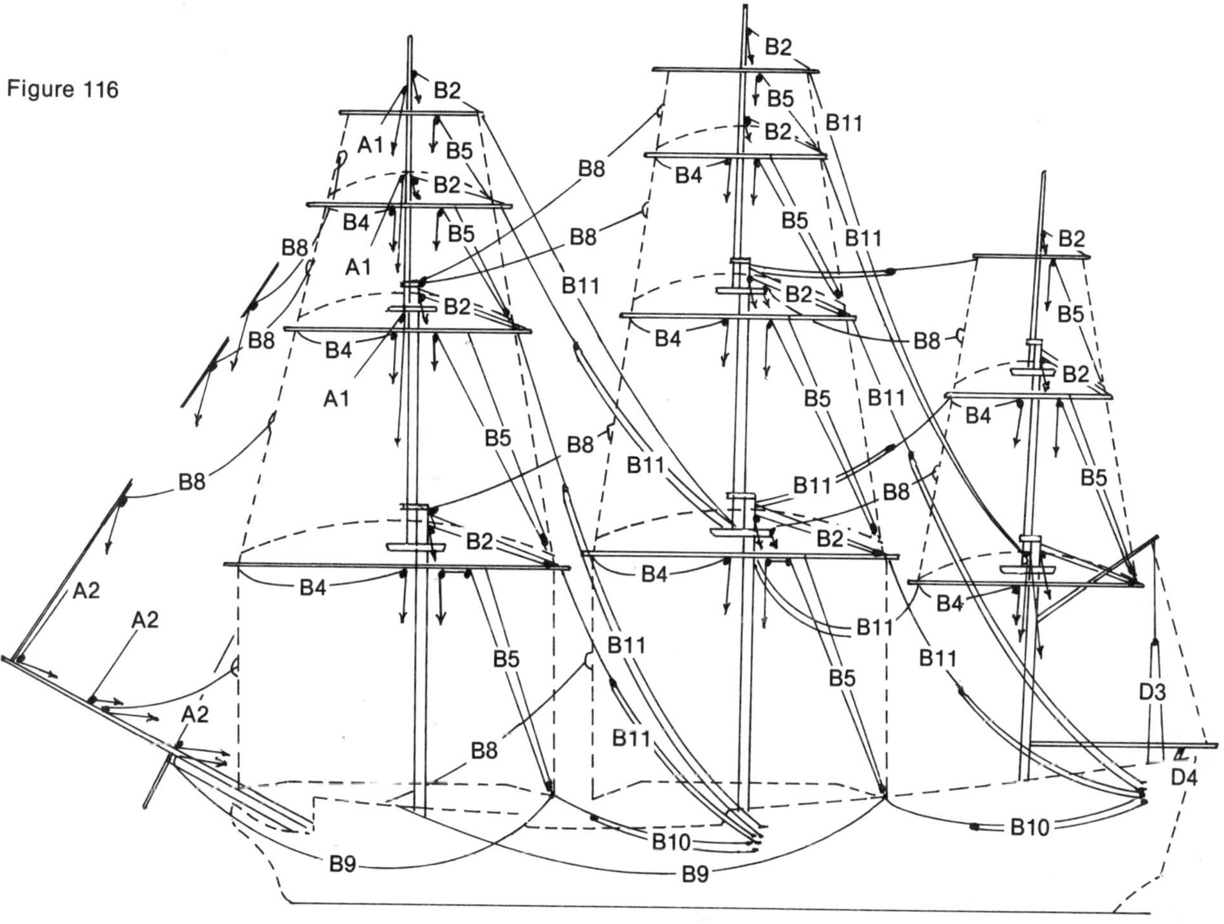

Figure 116

A. HEAD RIGGING
1. Halliards—work from inboard out
2. Down hauls— inhauls—work from inboard out
*3. Sheets not shown

B. SQUARE SAILS
1. Jeers, halliards, ties, slings, trusses not shown
2. Lifts
3. Bend sails
4. Upper Sheets—tie off on yard above with no sails
5. Clews/clew garnets—snug block to yard with no sails
*6. Buntlines not shown
*7. Leechlines not shown
*8. Bowlines
*9. Tack—one side only on lower courses. Delete sheet on side with tack.
*10. Lower sheets
*11. Braces—do not set up until all of the rest of the ship is rigged.

    Otherwise, they will block access to the pin rails, etc.

*12. Reef tackle not shown

C. STAYSAILS
1. Halliards not shown
2. Dowhauls, inhauls not shown
*3. Sheets not shown

D. SPANKER
1. Throat and peak halliards not shown
2. Topping lift not shown
3. Vangs
4. Sheet

E. STUNSAILS
1. Halliards not shown
*2. Tacks not shown
*3. Sheets not shown
*4. Braces not shown

BELAYING AND TYING OFF

Each line of a ship had its own belaying point, the place where it was made fast on deck, at the top or other place. Each ship had its own belaying pattern depending on its type, era, and the style of its captain. Many model plans include a chart of the ship's belaying points and should be used as the authority for the vessel in question.

A few general principles may be observed, however. First, the lines of the higher sails were tied off aft of those of lower sails, creating a fan pattern emanating from the mast tops more or less like the shrouds. Thus the principle "the higher the line, the further aft on the pin rail it is belayed."

From fore to aft the clews, bunts and leeches usually followed in sequence for each yard.

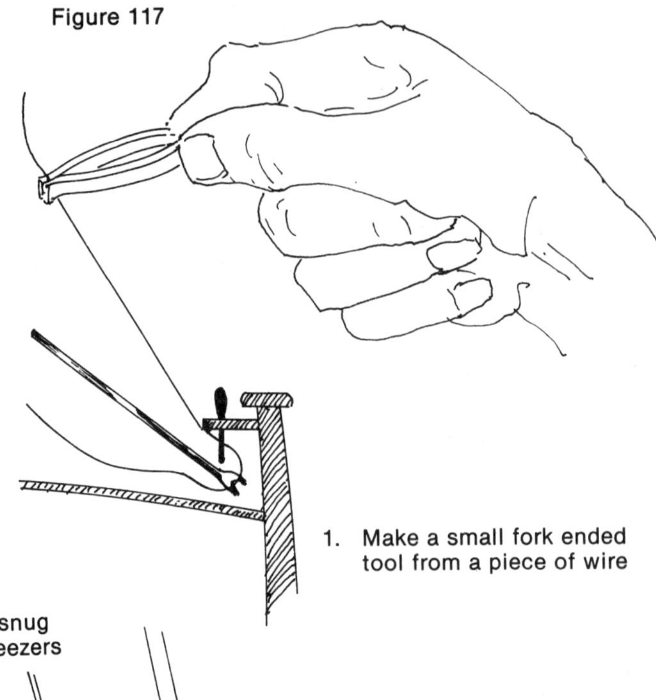

Figure 117

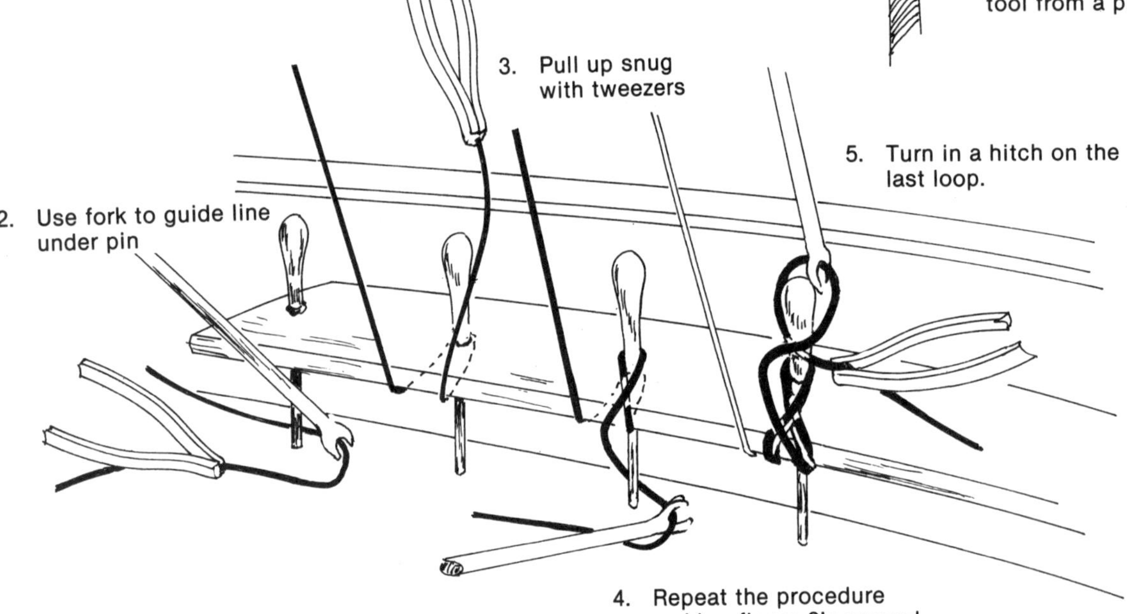

Figure 118

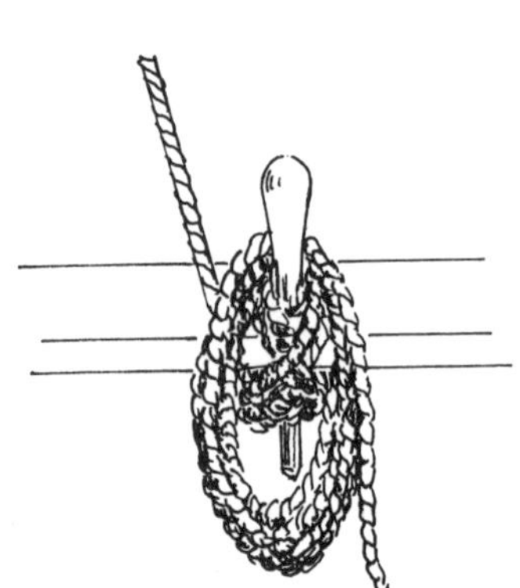

Coils look like this on the rail

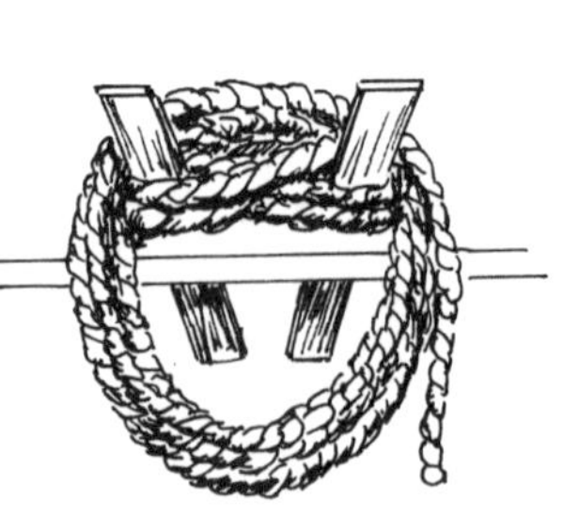

Coil on a kevel

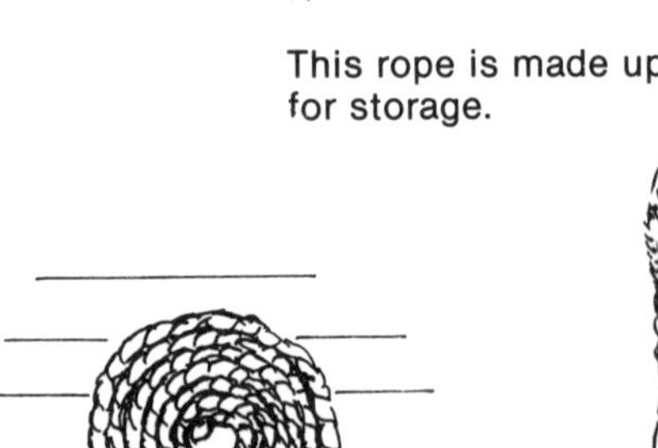

Larger lines may be made into flat coils

This rope is made up for storage.

54

MAKING SAILS Figure 119

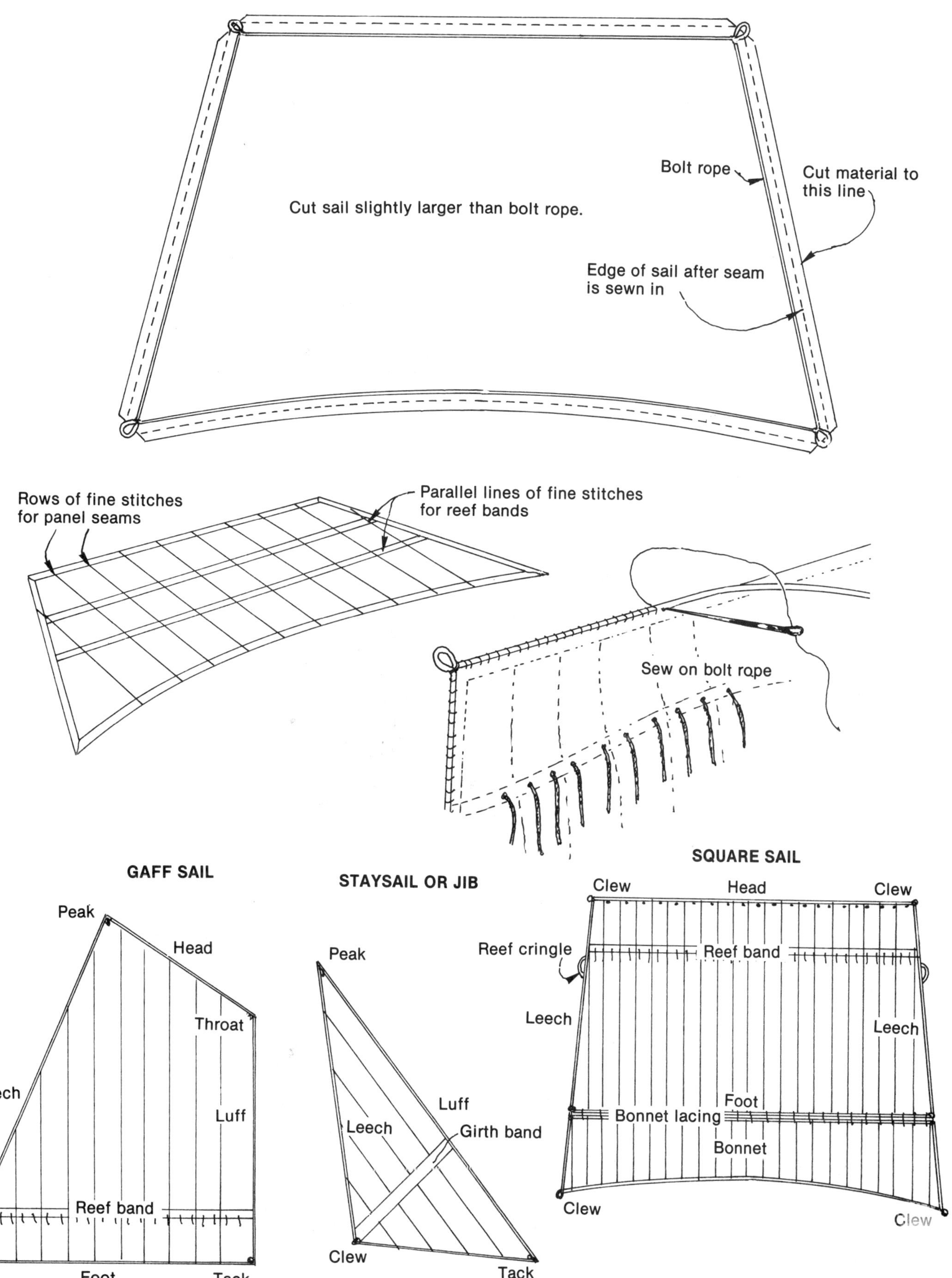

BENDING SAILS Figure 120

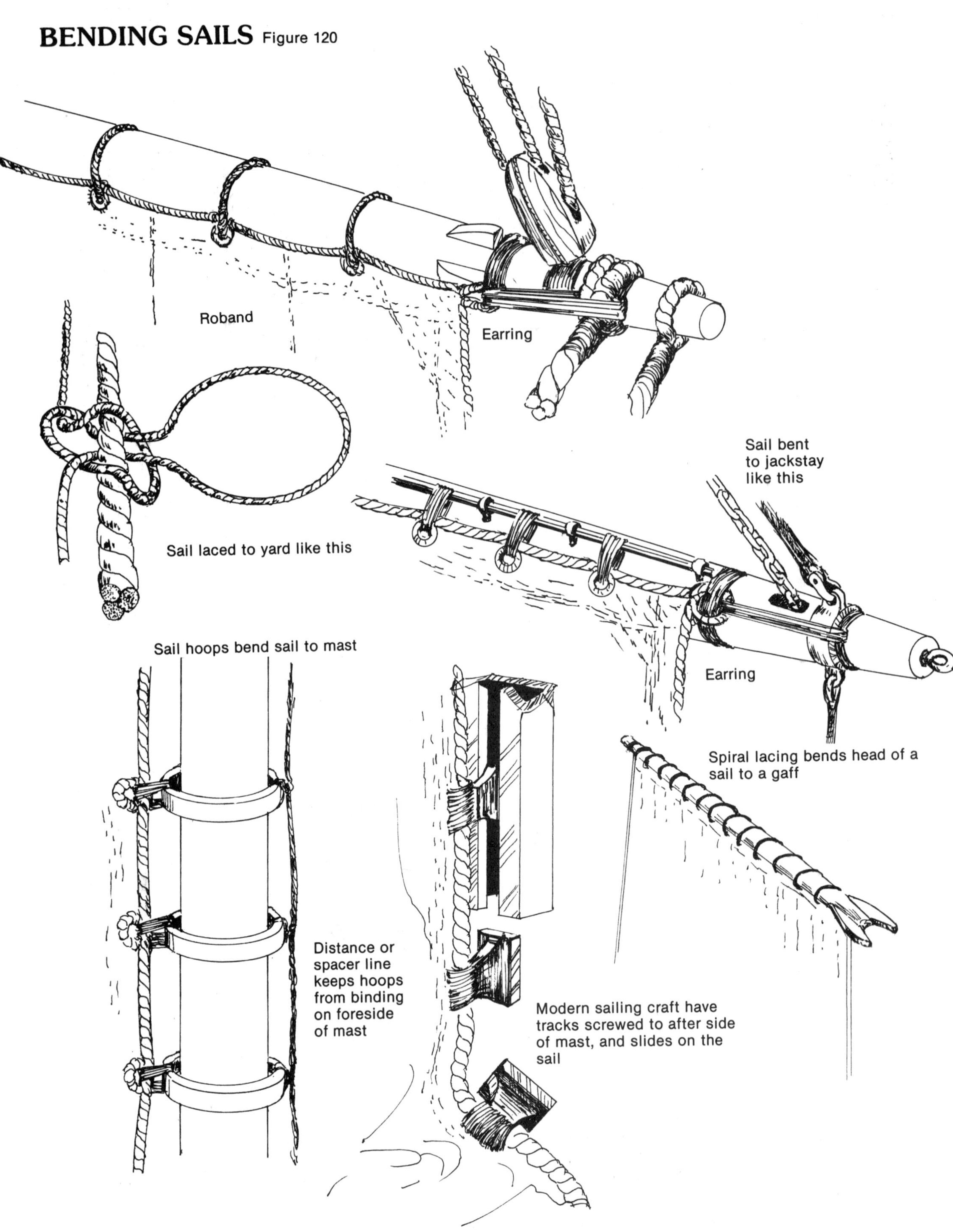

FINISHING TOUCHES

Touches that can add charm to a model are carved crewmen, personal gear, such as clothing hung out to dry: livestock (old timers shipped goats and pigs alive for fresh meat); small arms, and fishing tackle. The modeller can use his imagination here in making his ship come alive with human detail.

A pair of small cradles screwed to the base may be used to hold the model upright. Brass stanchions screwed to the base and to the keel are also effective, while some modellers like to build up a scale dry dock as a support.

The important point about support structures is to keep them simple and unobstrusive.

Display cases may be purchased or built from glass and wood or plexiglass. Leave vent holes near the bottom of the display case. A case works like a greenhouse. Heat builds up inside it and if the heat is not allowed to escape, it can warp and wreck your model in due time. For this reason, models should be displayed out of direct sunlight.

Small picture lights can be fitted for illumination.

An interesting trick that may be used to illuminate lanterns or below decks areas is the use of optical fibers. These fibers can "pipe" pin points of light perhaps equal to that of a scale candle from a hidden, outside source to appropriate places in the model.

MATERIALS AND TECHNICAL HINTS

Wood

A wide variety of wood is used in shipmodelling. Bass wood is perhaps most popular because it is fine grained, soft enough to work well yet hard enough to yield clean sharp edges and take a fine finish. Other woods that are often used are white pine, birch, mahogany, walnut, and fruit woods.

Bass, walnut and mahogany are available in hobby stores in small strips, sheets and blocks appropriate to model making. Strips and sheets may be obtained in thicknesses from 1/32" to 1/4". Kits contain wood stock of these small dimensions.

Birch dowels are often used for masts and other spars, though many modellers prefer the dependable straight grain of white pine for this purpose.

Fruit woods and other hard woods are sometimes selected by modellers for the variety of rich, natural finishes they afford. These stocks, however, must be purchased in standard board dimensions (1" x 2" etc.) For this reason, the beginner without power tools will probably prefer to stick with bass.

The important consideration in the choice of wood for a ship model is the size of the grain. Heavily grained wood such as oak appear grossly out of scale. A fine straight grained material is much more effective.

Balsa wood while familiar to all as a model airplane material, has limited application in ship modelling. The author has used balsa for out-of-sight components in the hull, and for molds. It is an unsatisfactory material for any superficial part of a ship model.

Metal

Brass, "white" metal, and Brittania metal are perhaps the three most commonly used metals in ship modelling.

Hobby shops carry brass in a variety of forms including wire, sheets of shim stock dimensions, tubing and other extrusions. Small brads, and screws are also available.

Many brass ship model fittings are also available as noted in the earlier pages of the book. Among these are anchors, steering wheels, capstans, cannon belaying pins, propellers, cleats and yard irons. Since the fabrication of many of these small intricate parts is quite challenging and time consuming the beginner is probably best advised to use these prefabricated fittings.

The same array of fittings is also available in white metal, a rather brittle alloy of lead.

The modeller wishing to make his own metal fittings can find the needed technical information in many of the books available on jewelry making. These handbooks often contain detailed descriptions of turning, casting, drawing, soldering, forging and the like of small metal parts.

Paints and Finishes

The finish of a ship model may be natural wood, or a paint job designed to match the finish of the real ship.

The natural wood finish is logical for old wooden sailing vessels, while the fine texture of the material and the wood craftsmanship add much to the charm of the finished model.

A painted finish is perhaps easier for the beginner in that paint can be used to camouflage blemishes in woodwork, paper and tape components and other elements that would have to be made of a "natural" material to look right without paint.

A matte or semi-matte finish on a ship model is to be preferred to a high gloss.

Artist's acrylic paints thin with water, dry quickly and can be made to yield very authentic looking paint jobs. Use red sable watercolor *sign painting* brushes with acrylics.

Artist's oil paints may also be used to good effect. Thin the paint with a mixture of ½ turpentine and ½ damar varnish and about 1 drop per ounce of cobalt dryer (siccatif). Mix up the thinner and dryer in a cup. Thin out the paint a brushful at a time by dipping the brush first into the medium and then into the paint blob on a palette. (an old plate will do). Use red sable *oil* painting brushes. Do not use watercolor brushes in oil paints. They will be ruined forever.

As a rule, each component of the model should be given its final finish before being fitted to the hull, and the hull finished completely before anything else is added to it.

TOOLS

A shipmodeller's tool chest eventually becomes extensive, including power tools and an assortment of homemade devices for various tasks.

The beginner, however, can get started with the following as recommended by Model Shipways:

"The Xacto No. 86 Hobby Chest—Contains the necessary knives, gouges, planes, and sanding aids to answer immediate needs.

Coping saw (or jeweler's saw frame) and fine blades
Razor, or "Zona", saw
Pointed tweezers
Needle files
Round-nose pliers
Flat-nose pliers (with serrated jaws)

The above can be bought at hobby shops which carry Xacto tools. Also needed, and to be had at hardware stores or machinist's supply houses:

Pin vise (4-collet swivel type or Starrett fixed-

collet type in two or three different sizes, including the smallest.)
Twist drills in sizes #60, 65, 70, and 75
Mill files (flat and half-round) in 8" and 10" lengths
Knife file, 6" or 8 ", the smaller the better
Small bench vise
Draftsman's dividers

The above tools are the minimum essentials and on which the more experienced craftsman could naturally improve. Let reasonable quality at modest price suffice until you are sure of your needs."

KIT MANUFACTURERS

Billing	**Mantua**
Blue Jacket	**Model Shipways**
Carta Augusto	**Moonraker**
Corel	**Scientific**
Fisher, A. J.	**Sergal**
Fusta	**Sterling**

The above manufacturers offer lines of wood ship model kits ranging in price from $25 or $30, to $1,000 or more. The price of a kit generally varies with 1) the number and type of pre-cast fittings; 2) scale and; 3) degree of authentic detail.

The beginner is advised to select a kit of comparatively large scale (¼" to the foot) and simple rig. Small scale models contain such small components they are difficult to see and frequently employ modelling stylizations, such as beads for blocks.

Plastic Kits

There are another number of kits on the market in which all of the parts are of preformed plastic. These kits are comparatively inexpensive and contain a fair amount of authentic information. They are comparatively simple to assemble and require few tools. The beginner may find one of these kits a good stepping stone into the art, though the finished effect of such a model is no match for a fine wood and metal creation. Plastic kits contain easy to follow step-by-step instruction booklets.

SOURCES OF PLANS AND INFORMATION

Some kit manufacturers market the plans of their kits as separate items. These plans are available at small expense through hobby stores or may be obtained by contacting the manufacturer directly.

Your local library is the best place to start looking for plans. There are many books which contain detailed drawings of all sorts of ships and sometimes feature drawings large enough to work from directly.

Undersized drawings from books can sometimes be blown up to working size by a photostat process. A glance at your telephone directory yellow pages under "photostats" or "reprographic services" can tell you where to get blow-ups done in your neighborhood.

The Smithsonian Institute in Washington, D.C. has a giant collection of plans of American built ships from the Revolutionary period forward. Write to Curator of Transportation, Smithsonian Institute, Washington, D.C. 20560.

The National Maritime Museum, Greenwich, England provides plans of English vessels, while most European countries have similar maritime archives.

Maritime museums generally are useful sources of not only plans but much other information as well. Here are some of the museums with nautical offerings in the United States:

Addison Gallery of Art, Andover, Mass.
Atwater Kent Museum, Philadelphia, Penn.
Boston Marine Museum, Boston, Mass.
Boston Museum of Fine Arts, Boston, Mass.
Buffalo Historical Society, Buffalo, New York
Chesapeake Bay Maritime Museum,
St. Michaels, Md.
Francis Russel Hart Nautical Museum,
Cambridge, Mass.
Franklin D. Roosevelt Memorial Library,
Hyde Park, New York
Franklin Institute, Philadelphia, Penn.
Great Lakes Museum, Detroit, Michigan
Kennebec Valley Marine Museum, Bath, Maine
Mariners Museum, Newport News, Virginia
Museum of the City of New York, New York,
New York
Museum of Science and Industry, Chicago,
Illinois
Mystic Seaport, Mystic, Connecticutt
Nantucket Whaling Museum, Nantucket,
Massachusetts
Naval Historical Foundation,
Washington, D. C.
New York Historical Society, New York,
New York
Peabody Museum, Salem, Massachusetts
Queen Mary Museum, Long Beach, California
River Museum (The), Marietta, Ohio
San Francisco Maritime Museum,
San Francisco, California
South Street Seaport, New York, New York
Star of India, San Diego, California
U.S. Maritime Commission, Washington, D. C.
U.S. Merchant Marine Academy, Kings Point,
New York
U.S. Naval Academy, Annapolis, Maryland
U.S. Navy Department, Washington, D. C.

A number of periodical publications also contain plans or advertise their availability. Among these are:

The National Fisherman
The Nautical Research Journal,
Washington, D. C.
The Fife Rail, Chicago, Illinois
Model Boats, Hertshire, England
Steamboat Bill, Staten Island, New York

GLOSSARY AND INDEX

SOURCES

Abell, Sir Westcott
The Shipwright's Trade
Cambridge, Massachusetts, 1948

Anderson, R. C.
Seventeenth Century Rigging
Hemel Hempstead, Herts, 1955

Baker, W. A.
The Development of Wooden Ship Construction
Quincy, Massachusetts, 1955

Campbell, G. F.
Jackstay
Bogota, New Jersey, 1962

Charnock, J.
History of Marine Architecture
London, 1802

Davis, C. G.
Ships of the Past
New York, 1929
Ship Model Builder's Assistant
New York (reprint) 1970

Haws, Duncan
Ships and the Sea
Gothenburg, Swede, 1975

Landstrom, Bjorn
The Ship
Stockholm and London, 1961

Nordbok, A. B. et al
The Lore of Ships
Gothenburg, Sweden, 1975

Ronnberg, Jr., Erick A. R.
Benjamin W. Latham
Bogota, New Jersey, 1973

Underhill, Harold A.
Sailing Ships and Rigging
Glasgow, 1938

Webster, F. B.
Shipbuilding Cyklopedia
New York, 1920

ON THE COVER

Ted Whomsley's first ship modeling project was the Eighteenth Century bomb ketch, *Racehorse,* scale 3/16″ = 1′ - 0″. He achieved this excellent result from a Sergal kit. Ted exercised some poetic license in his rendering of the ship which sticklers for authenticity could criticize, but how handsome she is!

The *Racehorse* was originally a 385-ton French Privateer christened the *Marquis de Vaudreuil,* launched about 1750. The British captured her during the Seven Years War.

In 1773, she and a consort, the *Carcass,* sailed on an Arctic expedition in an unsuccessful attempt to find the North-east Passage from Europe to China over the top of Russia.

Captured by the Americans during the Revolution, the Royal Navy finally blew her apart during a 1777 engagement in Delaware Bay.